Anita Forlines

MAKE
YOUR
TEACHING
COUNT!

MAKE YOUR TEACHING COUNT!

WESLEY R. WILLIS

VICTOR BOOKS®

A DIVISION OF SCRIPTURE PRESS PUBLICATIONS INC.
USA CANADA ENGLAND

Unless otherwise noted, Scripture quotations are
from the *New American Standard Bible*, © the
Lockman Foundation 1960, 1962, 1963, 1968,
1971, 1972, 1973, 1975, 1977. Other quotations are
from the *King James Version* (KJV).

Fourth printing, 1989

Recommended Dewey Decimal Classification: 268.6
Suggested Subject Heading: RELIGIOUS TRAINING
AND INSTRUCTION, METHODS OF INSTRUCTION AND STUDY

Library of Congress Catalog Card Number: 85-50312
ISBN: 0-89693-324-5

VICTOR BOOKS
A division of SP Publications, Inc.
Wheaton, Illinois 60187

CONTENTS

CHAPTER ONE
WHAT'S SO IMPORTANT ABOUT SUNDAY SCHOOL, ANYWAY?

"Sunday School stinks!" the young girl vehemently declared.

"Sunday School is my very most favorite time of the whole week," another child stated.

Both children had just been asked what they thought of their Sunday School classes. As their responses clearly indicate, the subject of Sunday School is capable of producing a wide range of responses.

Some children complain that there's never anything new in their Church School classes. They feel that teachers repeat the same old stories, week after week, year after excruciatingly dull year. Several weeks ago, in fact, one of the sixth-grade boys whom I teach at our church told me he had studied the same lesson (the one I was about to teach) every year for the last three years. Though I suspected he was wrong, there was no question in his mind that he was about to be subjected to another Sunday morning of dreary repetition.

Other children and adults, however, would not miss Sunday School for anything. The time they spend studying the Bible

7

and relating to fellow students is cherished time. They seek to understand the meaning of the Bible in order to serve God as He wishes. Students in such classes go to bed on Saturday night excited because the next day is Sunday. Church School is the highlight of their week.

This range of feelings about Sunday School often seems to vary as much among teachers as it does among students. Some teachers clearly love their work. Last week a retired Sunday School teacher showed me a card she had received from a former student. The student, now an adult, wrote to say how much this particular teacher had influenced her. She indicated that many of the lessons learned years earlier in a Junior High class continued to guide her behavior today. This one note really made my friend's day.

Other teachers, though, apparently view their Sunday School involvement as little more than a necessary evil. I heard one teacher say she hated teaching her class; she was delighted each week when it ended. But then she would become depressed, knowing that next week, she'd have yet another class to endure.

Likewise, while visiting a church, I once asked one member if she taught any Sunday School classes. She replied that she had "put in her time" years ago and was finished with all that now. She sounded like an ex-convict who had spent years in prison. That part of her life was past, and she had no intention of returning—ever!

Undoubtedly, the quality of Sunday School experiences varies widely. Some are positive and others negative. Some classes have influenced students profoundly, while others have been forgotten almost immediately. And with this variation in experience, opinions also vary widely as to the importance of Sunday School today.

This book is written under the assumption that Sunday School should be a *positive* experience. Indeed, I'm assuming that if a person has a deep desire to plan and conduct an effective Sunday School class, the battle for quality Christian education is mostly won.

The purpose of this book is to assist any person—teacher or administrator—who wants to participate in a profitable, exciting Christian education experience. Some of the recommendations included in this book are based on my own experience in teaching and administrating Christian education programs. But the information presented here goes beyond my own experiences. It includes valuable suggestions and illustrations from many other sources to guide you as a Sunday School teacher or administrator.

A Brief History
of the Sunday School Movement

Recently, a Christian educator approached me with a question. "What's so important about Sunday School, anyway?" he asked. "Can't we accomplish the same things through other programs?" He was implying that church education is a program devised by man, one not directly commanded by God. Therefore, because Sunday School is a human institution, it can be replaced by some alternate program.

Of course, his implication that Sunday School is an earthly Christian education program is correct. The Sunday School movement, as we know it, was begun in 1780. Gloucester, England was the place, and Robert Raikes, a newspaper publisher, was the prime mover. Raikes concluded that something had to be done to break the vicious cycle of poverty and crime then existing in his country. So he began working with adult prisoners. However, after several years, Raikes turned his attention to children, most of whom were abused and illiterate.

Since lower-class children worked six days a week, Sunday was the only day available for instruction. Accordingly, Raikes began a school that met every Sunday to teach children to read and write. After they knew how to read, Raikes took them to church to worship; he reasoned that if children knew how to read, they could study the Bible and the Catechism and learn to obey God. So he taught the children in his school on Sundays.

From this early beginning, the Sunday School movement swept around the world. By the early 1800s, such schools were a vital agency of religious education in this country. In the more established eastern parts of the United States, Sunday Schools generally followed the British pattern; they met on Sunday afternoon in a church building or a home. Farther west, Sunday Schools often were the *only* available form of religious instruction. Traditionally, they met in homes or in public buildings.

Before long, however, most Sunday Schools in America were incorporated into existing churches. In frontier towns, where Sunday Schools sometimes were started even before churches were founded, those schools usually grew into full-fledged churches. This long tradition of combining Sunday School with other church programs is one of the reasons the movement has maintained its vitality in the United States. By the beginning of the twentieth century, most churches included both a worship service and a Sunday School.

A morning worship service probably is the most common program element found in Protestant churches. Almost all churches schedule at least one meeting each week, usually on Sunday morning, for the purpose of corporate worship. This service includes a sermon from the Bible or about biblical principles, and exhorts worshipers to live lives that are pleasing to God.

In addition to these regularly scheduled worship services, most churches also include Sunday Schools for the purpose of instruction. If a worship service is the most common feature of church life, Sunday School ordinarily is the second most common activity.

Unfortunately, in many churches, both the worship service *and* the Sunday School need revitalization. The mere fact that both of these programs have long been a standard part of church life is not reason enough to justify their continued existence. They must be fulfilling the body of Christ's divine mission: to win people to Him. To help accomplish this mission it would seem well worth the effort to plan church and Sunday School programs so as to gain the maximum value from them.

This book will suggest ways to improve the effectiveness of your church's Sunday School program. More specifically, we will consider ways to bolster the local church's teaching ministry. Application of the principles included in this book will enable administrators to plan more effective programs and will help instructors to teach students more skillfully.

No book can transform a teacher. But God can work in the life and experience of any person dedicated to Him. A teacher who wishes to teach more effectively can profit from the principles included in the following chapters. The net result will be an increase in learning, and greater enjoyment for both teachers and students throughout the teaching/learning process.

Prepared to Teach?

Not too many nights ago, I was out driving by myself. Suddenly, a wave of nostalgia washed over me. Recollections of college days and courting, seminary classes, and door-to-door sales to pay tuition bills flooded my memory. What set off this tidal wave of remembrances? Would you believe it all started when I pulled up behind a 1954 Ford? You see, that was the first type of car I ever owned; it was an integral part of my personality—a little bit strange, but very lovable. When I finally had to sell it due to a terminal case of galloping rust, I felt as though a part of me was gone forever.

But not all of my memories of that '54 Ford are exactly warm and fuzzy. Since I began driving it when I was in high school—a time during which I had no money for repairs—I was faced with the option of either fixing the car myself, or not driving it at all. This particular arrangement spawned some very interesting experiences. Take a tune-up, for example. Changing spark plugs is a relatively minor task. It should take only a few minutes. But in my case, changing six plugs often took as long as two hours! That sounds ridiculous, but there's really a very simple explanation for it.

The first problem was, I didn't know what I was doing! No one had ever told me that you shouldn't try to remove spark plugs from a hot engine. Since metal expands when it's hot, the plugs get so tight that even a Samson couldn't remove them.

A second problem was that I didn't have the right tools. No one in his right mind would try to remove a spark plug without using a socket wrench. At least that's my opinion today. But back then, an open-end wrench was my tool of choice. As a result, many frustrating, bruising, knuckle-busting hours were spent in the simple task of removing and replacing six spark plugs. I'm sure that some of the scars on my hands bear mute testimony to the early mechanic experiences I endured.

What does this story have to do with Sunday School? Well, how many inadequately equipped Sunday School teachers face similar frustrations? These teachers may have been appointed to their task for a wide variety of expedient—and questionable—reasons; now, they're suffering for it.

A person with a worn cover on his Bible, for instance, may have been adjudged a serious student of the Word. Obviously, he'd make a good teacher. (Of course, he may simply have been using his mother's Bible.) Then there's the substitute who's asked to fill in for "one Sunday." After seventeen years of teaching, she wonders if this is going to become a permanent job. Another teacher recounted that her teaching career began because she arrived late for church one Sunday morning. She was the only person in the hallway when the Sunday School superintendent realized he was short one teacher. He spotted her, and a teacher was born!

It's clear that these teachers were appointed for all the wrong reasons. No one evaluated their competency for teaching. Their spiritual gifts were not considered and specific teaching skills were not required of them. Is it any wonder that lay teachers experience so much frustration in our Sunday Schools and other Christian education programs?

What's even worse is that such recruits rarely are given training once they *have* been appointed to teach. Some become better teachers through trial and error. But they and their students probably will get bruised in the process. The result? Classes often are staffed with dedicated, well-intentioned, untrained teachers—teachers who *want* to do a good job, but who are limited by inadequate or nonexistent preparation.

The problem is that we generally fail to provide teachers with the proper tools they need to succeed. These include classrooms, equipment, teaching supplies, quality curriculum, and other resources. It's all but impossible to change spark plugs with an open-end wrench. But we often ask Sunday School teachers to attempt similarly impossible tasks in their classrooms.

This book is designed to help those who are teaching (or who think they might like to try) do a better job. Initially, this means analyzing what teachers should be trying to accomplish. A description of what teaching is all about, and an explanation of why teaching is so important, comprise a significant portion of this book. If we who are teachers understand the implications of teaching, and determine what we are trying to accomplish, there is a much higher probability of success.

Those who understand the goals and process of teaching also need to use the correct tools in order to teach more effectively. Some of those tools will be described in this book, while others will come from suggested resource books. The skillful use of such tools will help any teacher accomplish his or her important commission from God.

I've no doubt that anyone whom God has called to teach can become a good teacher. While there is no such thing as an "instant teacher," an understanding of what teaching is all about, and knowing how to use the tools of teaching, can lead to improvements in the classroom. Now, about changing those spark plugs in my car. . . .

Application Activities

Questions will be found at the end of each chapter to help you personalize the material you've just read. It would be even more profitable if you discussed your answers with fellow teachers.

(1) In the space below, describe a time when you tried to accomplish something, or perform some task, without adequate instruction.

---

(2) How did you feel when you were trying to fulfill that assignment? How do you feel about that experience now?

_____

_____

_____

(3) What could have been done at the time to improve that situation?

_____

_____

_____

(4) Why do you think we are prone to recruit unqualified teachers to teach in our Sunday Schools?

_____

_____

_____

(5) Since we often *do* assign poorly equipped teachers to teaching positions, why do you think we fail to give them more help after they begin teaching?

_____

_____

_____

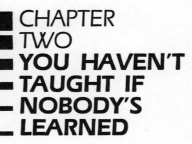

CHAPTER TWO
YOU HAVEN'T TAUGHT IF NOBODY'S LEARNED

Let's play a game. It's a word game, and it's fun! No, it's not Scrabble; and it's not a crossword puzzle. It's a word association game. I mention a word and you say the first thing that comes to mind. Got the idea? Great. Let's try "vacation." Very good. I imagine most of the words you thought of were positive. Unless, of course, the vacation you recalled was similar to a recent one of mine. My family and I drove almost 2,000 miles at Christmastime. Most of it was through snow (blizzard-like, that is), ice, sleet, and freezing rain. And two of our three boys got sick. Oh, you've had some vacations like that too, have you?

How about another word, "diet." Whoops! Sorry about that!

Why don't we move along to "Sunday School"? You probably had a variety of responses here. Some may have been positive, others negative. When I think of Sunday School, I'm reminded of the many wonderful people who loved and taught me as a child, and of many good experiences. Unfortunately, some children who respond to the phrase "Sunday School" come up with words such as "dull," "boring," "out-of-date," and the particularly descriptive, "yuck." But it doesn't have to be that way. The teaching/learning process can be a delightful, stimulating experience. And once a person has grasped the sense of accomplishment and satisfaction that comes from learning, he or she will never be the same again.

The Importance of Teaching

As indicated above, some students view formal learning experiences in a negative light. Consider this note (retrieved from a wastebasket) written by an eighth-grade student in Philadelphia:

> Dear Max, I don't know what's keeping you awake. I'm so bored I could stretch out and fall asleep. Do you believe she can stand there and talk so long? I wish she'd let us talk once in a while.

I guess we've all known students like Max's friend. Maybe some of *us* were that type of student. It's unfortunate when someone has a negative view of learning. It's even more regrettable when a student who hated learning becomes a teacher who *still* thinks learning is an unpleasant experience. Perhaps some of us fit into that category. But even if our learning experiences *were* negative and classes boring, when we teach we can impart a new vitality to our efforts. Several principles are worth noting in this respect.

For one, teaching should never bore the learner. I'm quite certain Jesus didn't have followers who dreaded His instruction. In fact, they even went without food in order to learn from Him. Jesus responded to their desire with true compassion:

> I feel compassion for the multitude, because they have remained with Me now three days and have nothing to eat; and I do not wish to send them away hungry (Matt. 15:32).

We who are teaching today should feel the same type of compassion for our learners. We should experience a compassion that extends to all aspects of our relationship with them. We should be concerned for students as persons. We should seek their comfort. And we should commit ourselves to helping learners love to attend class, to delight in learning eternal truth. In short, we should be deeply concerned about becoming excellent teachers.

Now I am not promising that if you study this book you'll have students who are so excited about learning that they'd give up eating to hear you teach. But you *can* become a *better* teacher. And your students will not describe your classes as "yuck." You will begin to grasp the wonder of the privilege of cooperating with the Holy Spirit in helping learners come to grips with vital and life-changing truths.

Transformed lives is what Sunday School teaching is all about. The most important reason I can think of for giving so much attention to teaching is that it is very important to God. Deuteronomy contains a key passage that can help us understand the significance He attaches to instruction:

> [1]Now this is the commandment, the statutes and the judgments which the Lord your God has commanded me to teach you, that you might do them in the land where you are going over to possess it, [2]so that you and your son and your grandson might fear the Lord your God, to keep all His statutes and His commandments, which I command you, all the days of your life, and that your days may be prolonged. [3]O Israel, you should listen and be careful to do it, that it may be well with you and that you may multiply greatly, just as the Lord, the God of your fathers, has promised you, in a land flowing with milk and honey. [4]Hear, O Israel! The Lord is our God, the Lord is One! [5]And you shall love the Lord your God with all your heart and with all your soul and

with all your might. ⁶And these words, which I am com-
manding you today, shall be on your heart; ⁷and you shall
teach them diligently to your sons and shall talk of them
when you sit in your house and when you walk by the way
and when you lie down and when you rise up. ⁸And you
shall bind them as a sign on your hand and they shall be as
frontals on your forehead. ⁹And you shall write them on the
doorposts of your houses and on your gates (Deut. 6:1-9).

As the Israelites prepared to enter the Promised Land, God
gave them a specific warning. He told them in no uncertain
terms that the only way to experience long life and prosperity
was for the leaders to teach the people to obey the laws of God
(v. 1).

The fifth and sixth verses of this passage, therefore, are specifically addressed to teachers. Those who teach must totally
love God (v. 5) and obey His commands (v. 6). Effective teaching can result only when these conditions are met. As for
methods, teachers are to use verbal presentations of the truth
(v. 7), visual demonstrations (v. 8), and everyday surroundings
(v. 9). As the Word of God was taught effectively among the
Israelites, the way God intended, consistent godly living would
result.

Unfortunately, the Jews failed to fully obey these guidelines.
The Book of Judges describes the result of that failure:

And all that generation also were gathered to their fathers;
and there arose another generation after them who did not
know the Lord, nor yet the work which He had done for
Israel. Then the sons of Israel did evil in the sight of the
Lord, and served the Baals (Jud. 2:10-11).

The same danger confronts us today. If we do not teach
God's truth, the generation following us may well turn its back

on God. It has been said that Christianity is always one generation away from extinction. While that may be something of an
overstatement, it does contain an important element of truth.
We are obligated to teach God's Word. If we fail, countless
lives will suffer irreparable loss. Teaching is a great joy and
privilege. But it also is a great responsibility to which God has
called us. May we be faithful to that calling.

The Nature of Teaching

In recent years, educational psychologists have devoted a great
deal of attention to the subject of learning. Many researchers
feel that the desire to learn actually is one of the most basic of
human drives.

If we want to understand this drive to learn, we need only to
watch infants. They're not content to lie around. They want to
roll over. And when they can do that, they're satisfied, right?
Not on your life! Then they want to crawl, and sit up, and
stand, and walk, and run and climb, always trying to do more
and better—for the rest of their lives! You see, God created us
with a drive to learn, to accomplish, to grow.

Unfortunately, this natural drive is stunted when the learning
process is perceived as boring, uninteresting, or unrelated to
life. Sitting in a classroom under a teacher's poorly designed
instruction is exactly the type of environment which can di-
vorce learning from life; misguided teaching fails to apply the
subject matter to the learner's needs.

People don't hate learning. If they hate anything, they hate
being taught lessons which seem to have little bearing on their
interests and needs. Learning is unpleasant only if it seems
useless or irrelevant. But God has not called us to that kind of
teaching. He expects us to teach in such a way that true learning occurs. In short, until learning has occurred, we have not
taught. Some time ago, a friend met me in church and asked if
I had taught a Sunday School class that morning. "I don't

know," I replied. "It all depends on whether or not anyone learned."

A brief look at some words used in the Old Testament to describe teaching and learning may help us understand these concepts more clearly.

Old Testament Teaching/Learning Terms

Four Hebrew words are commonly used in Scripture to describe teaching. These are *lamad* (to teach), *yada* (to know), *bin* (to distinguish or understand), and *zahar* (to warn).

Lamad is the Hebrew word most commonly associated with the teaching/learning process. Originally, it referred to goading an ox to get him moving. It later came to emphasize getting someone to know something. *Lamad* really means "to cause to learn," which is a clear indication that biblical teaching cannot be separated from learning. As I mentioned a moment ago, we who claim to be teachers have not taught until someone has learned—and the concept of *lamad* drives this truth home.

An example of this word is found in Deuteronomy: "You shall *teach (lamad)* them, that they may observe them" (5:31, italics and addition mine). Please notice that the laws of God were to be taught not as abstract knowledge, but with an application to daily life.

Yada describes such a deep level of understanding that it is the word generally used in the Old Testament to describe sexual intimacy. *Yada* is used in Joshua, however, to describe Israel's response to God's direction: "That you may *know (yada)* the way by which you shall go" (3:4, italics and addition mine). Here God communicated and gave direction to Israel through the ark of the covenant. When the ark was carried forward, it communicated God's will; that knowledge enabled the nation to resume its journey. Knowledge led to action.

Bin first meant "to separate," but as the Hebrew language developed, it came to mean "to distinguish" or "to understand." We read in Nehemiah that after the Jews rebuilt the wall of Jerusalem, "the Levites *caused* the people *to understand (bin)* the Law" (8:7, italics and addition mine, KJV). Today, some might refer to this concept as "heart knowledge" that leads to action, as opposed to "head knowledge," which is not applied to life.

Zahar is the fourth Hebrew word we will consider. •It originally meant "to shine a light upon," but later came to mean "to warn." In Ezekiel, the servant of God is commanded "*to warn (zahar)* the wicked from his wicked way, that he may live" (3:18, italics and addition mine). The purpose of a warning always is to promote action. The person who receives a warning must pay attention to it, otherwise it is in vain.

Has a teacher taught? Well, that all depends on whether or not the lesson has been learned. Valid teaching always leads to learning. God expects teachers to teach in a manner that enables students to learn. These four Hebrew words clearly attest to that fact.

Some years ago, when our three sons still were riding tricycles, I told them never to leave their bikes in the driveway behind a parked car. I went into great detail describing what would happen if I were to back up the car without knowing their tricycles were there. Had you asked me, I would have told you that I had effectively communicated this message to my sons. I might even have said I had taught them a thing or two. I genuinely thought I had!

One day, though, as I was starting to back out of the driveway, I heard a sickening crunch. An anxious investigation confirmed my fears. There, partly under the car, was a twisted, broken tricycle. I was furious. After all, hadn't I taught my sons not to leave their trikes there? But then, a thought occurred to me. In all honesty, I realized I really had not *taught* my sons anything. I merely had *told* them something. No real learning had taken place; the fact that a broken tricycle now rested under my car proved that point. It was a costly lesson, but it showed me a great deal about the true meaning of the teaching/learning process.

New Testament Teaching/Learning Words

Thankfully, we don't *have* to learn through broken bikes. We can pay attention to instruction. Someone has said that Experience may be the best teacher; the problem is, she gives the exams before she teaches the lessons! God expects teachers to teach in such a way that learners can be spared the painful results of being taught by experience. The Greek words commonly used in the New Testament to describe the teaching/learning process amply demonstrate that paying attention to instruction is better than suffering experience's painful lessons. The terms we will consider are *didasko* (to teach), *noutheteo* (to admonish), *paideuo* (to train), and *matheteuo* (to make a disciple).

Diadasko is used more than 100 times in the New Testament. Its meaning grows out of another word, *dao*, which means, "to learn." The very origin of *didasko* shows the close interaction between teaching a subject and applying it to life.

In his first letter to the Corinthians, Paul informed the believers at Corinth that they were to apply the principles of his teaching, "just as *I teach (didasko)* everywhere in every church" (4:17, italics and addition mine). This message was so important that Paul sent Timothy to deliver it personally. The Corinthians were to observe the way that Paul lived and imitate His example in following Christ (4:16). Today, even as then, instruction should lead to obedience, which results in godly Christian living.

Noutheteo actually is a combination of two words, *nous* (mind) and *titheni* (to put or place). Together, they literally mean, "to put into the mind." Since *noutheteo* usually is translated "to admonish," or "to instruct," Paul told parents to "bring [children] up in the discipline and *instruction (nouthete)* of the Lord" (Eph. 6:4, italics and addition mine).

While the previous word tends to emphasize warnings about what *not* to do, *paideuo* speaks of more positive instruction. It can be translated "to train," or "to nurture." The emphasis here is on providing positive direction. It means more than telling your son not to leave his bike behind the car. It means showing him a better place to store it. As the Apostle indicated, "All Scripture is inspired by God and is profitable . . . for *training (paideuo)* in righteousness" (2 Tim. 3:16, italics and addition mine). Biblical instruction always should result in changed behavior which leads to righteous living.

Matheteuo is the fourth word we'll mention in this section. The original word from which it is derived is *manthano* (to learn); the verb form emphasizes the process by which a person can become the disciple of his teacher. Thus, the followers of Jesus were His disciples because they learned from Him and were committed to following Him.

In considering these words, it is important to note the emphasis each places on actually putting into practice those things which have been taught. My son knew that he shouldn't leave his bike behind the car. And yet, in the biblical sense, he *didn't* know it. He realized I had told him what to do; when he laid his bike behind the car, he may even have thought, *I shouldn't put it there, but I'll come right back and get it before Dad backs up.* But my son really had not learned the intended lesson because he failed to translate that knowledge into action.

What Does It All Mean?

Have you ever noticed that many teachers set very short-range goals for their instruction? Some teachers seem to feel that just making it to the end of class is sufficient. Or perhaps they are satisfied if they're simply able to keep their students quiet. Other teachers may go a bit further. Their goal is "to cover the material." Unfortunately, this usually translates into "saying everything I wanted to say" with little regard for whether actual learning has taken place.

As the words we've just studied show, teaching must be more than filling the time, keeping students quiet, or even covering the material. Teaching must translate into life. Teaching must influence behavior for it to be truly valid instruction.

Most people are able to look back to significant events in their lives. Sometimes the course of an entire life is altered because of a particular relationship. That proved true in my experience. When I was a younger Christian, God provided several teachers whose ministries greatly enhanced my spiritual maturity. I suspect none of these teachers were aware of the powerful influence they exerted. But they were used of God to provide the instruction and the example I needed at that point in my life.

Always keep in mind as you prepare yourself to teach that God may give you the great privilege of being His appointed servant to reach into the life of a particular learner. Yes, it does take work to teach effectively. But it is a vital way to serve God. I pray that one day, some person will be able to think back to a particular time when God redirected his life. And I pray that *you* will be the channel through whom God worked.

Application Activities

(1) Who was the best teacher you ever had? Write down several key memories you recall about that teacher.

_____

_____

_____

_____

_____

_____

_____

(2) Now think of a negative learning experience you have had. Write down several memories which stand out in your mind from that experience.

_____

_____

_____

_____

_____

_____

_____

(3) What ideas do you have about teaching and learning as you reminisce over those learning experiences? Write down ideas that come to mind.

_____

_____

_____

_____

_____

_____

_____

_____

(4) Read each of the following Old Testament verses, and then write down the expected behavior you think might grow out of the lesson learned: Deuteronomy 4:35; 6:1; Psalms 19:11; 119:144.

_____

_____

_____

_____

_____

_____

_____

(5) Read each of the following New Testament verses and write down the behavior you expect to develop after the lesson has been taught/learned: Matthew 28:19-20; Romans 2:21; Colos-

sians 1:28; Titus 2:11-12.

_____

_____

_____

_____

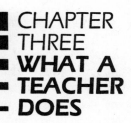

CHAPTER THREE
WHAT A TEACHER DOES

Our family has stored up many delightful memories from the various camping trips we've taken through the years. One excursion we went on several years ago particularly stands out in my mind.

My wife Elaine and I, along with our three sons, Mark, Kevin, and Nathan, spent almost a week canoeing the Boundary Waters region of northern Minnesota. This wilderness area is ideally suited for such activities. Though natural and unspoiled, it is well charted and relatively safe (just don't ask Elaine about the bear she saw).

Because trips into the Boundary Waters are not particularly hazardous, most groups traveling there do not need a guide. With a reliable outfitter, good maps, and some wilderness proficiency, most canoeists can handle the experience by themselves.

There are other areas of the world, however, such as the Himalayas, where having a seasoned guide is a matter of life and death. Imagine we're exploring that dangerous area and our guide—whom we've never met before—comes out to greet us. After exchanging initial pleasantries, he begins to speak of the region we're about to visit. Our guide tells us he's never been there before—but assures us it's beautiful. Oh, yes, he mentions, it's true we'll encounter some potentially dangerous situations, but he doesn't think we'll experience any real problems—at least he hopes not; after all, he doesn't have a first-aid kit.

By the time this alleged guide asks if anyone in our group has a map and compass he can borrow, the picture has become very clear. This man is not qualified to be a member of our group, let alone guide us. Needless to say, our plans change on the spot. If we still want to explore the area, we will hire a *trained* guide. No group wants a leader who is inexperienced, unskilled, and unprepared.

Giving Guidance to Learners

In many ways, a Sunday School teacher is similar to a guide. A guide must be well acquainted with the area a group's planning to explore before he can help others discover it. And ultimately, the guide's value is determined by how well he helps others enjoy a proper experience—be that hiking or canoeing.

Likewise, what a Sunday School teacher does takes on meaning only if learners have positive experiences which produce desired results. Learning is an activity which a teacher clearly can encourage and promote. But that teacher cannot learn *for* his or her students. Students, themselves must learn and develop; the teacher only can encourage and enable them.

In seminars that I conduct for Christian educators, I have Sunday School teachers participate in a variety of activities. In one, I ask them to discuss how teaching is similar to certain other vocations; specifically, I ask teachers to indicate which occupation they think most resembles teaching. I provide them a list which includes: preacher, lecturer, policeman, animal trainer, group leader, explorers' guide, news commentator, and sculptor. Usually, they vote for "guide" and "sculptor." The term "guide" obviously is a good choice—in light of the points we've considered above.

However, I am troubled by the fact that many people think Sunday School teaching is similar to sculpting. I say this because such a response implies that the *teacher's* work is what really matters in the education process. True, in teaching, an element of sculpting does exist—but not because a teacher serves as the sculptor. Rather, the true sculptor is God; a teacher simply is a tool in His hand.

Some grave misconceptions can arise if a teacher perceives of himself as a sculptor. This viewpoint suggests, for instance, that a teacher has absolute authority over the outcome of the teaching/learning process, just as a real sculptor has authority over his slab of marble. We all know that this is not the case. Students have minds of their own and must make their own decisions. While a teacher certainly can play a significant role in helping guide the learner toward good decisions, each student must decide for himself what he will or will not believe and do.

The teacher-as-sculptor school of thought also assumes that every teacher knows exactly how his student should develop, and that he knows precisely how to sculpt the learner in that direction. After all, a sculptor can't begin his work unless he knows beforehand what he wants to create and knows what tools to use. Prospective Sunday School teachers should recognize, though, that they do not need profound insight or manipulative ability to be effective educators. All they need is a willingness to be used of God for their students' benefit.

So what *is* teaching, then? In the final analysis, teaching might be best described as an activity that promotes learning. Yet a teacher can do this only if he also continues to learn. What does that mean? Well, as a teacher discovers God's truth and applies it in his own life, only then is he in a position to help others learn. Thus, rather than trying to be the source of all wisdom and knowledge, a teacher's prime obligation is to guide the learner through the teaching/learning process; the student's responsibility is to learn.

Teaching through Example

Recently, a friend of mine described a conversation he had with his teenage son. My friend needed to confess a sin to his son and to ask his forgiveness. Needless to say, he was somewhat anxious about doing this.

"Will my son understand?" he asked. "Will he forgive me? What will his attitude be toward me in the future?" In spite of his fear and misgiving, this father finally went ahead and asked his son for forgiveness.

When the son heard his father's statement and request, his response was revealing: "Dad, do you remember last summer when I confessed that I had lied to you? You forgave me and embraced me. How could I do anything less now?"

I was glad to hear that the situation was resolved in this fashion. For under a different set of circumstances, the results could have been devastating. Suppose that the father had bitterly condemned his son for lying. What if he had been harsh, unloving, and insensitive? His son probably would have responded in a similar manner. But my friend had modeled Christian love and forgiveness. As a result, his son learned the lesson well, and we all praised God.

Sunday School teachers also teach by modeling, which is why Paul challenged Timothy to live a godly life—to teach by example.

Prescribe and teach these things. Let no one look down on your youthfulness, but rather in speech, conduct, love, faith and purity, show yourself an example of those who believe (1 Tim. 4:11-12).

A teacher first must *be* what he would teach—which is why a teacher who is not a good learner cannot be a good teacher, either. Only as we learn the lessons that God teaches us can we serve as models for our students. Teachers guide students and demonstrate truth in action for them. In short, they model Christian living.

Jesus' earthly ministry lasted only three years. Yet in that short time, He prepared a select group of followers to carry on His work after His ascension. Needless to say, what Christ did in those three years was crucial. He had to take a small band of individuals with a wide variety of backgrounds and knowledge, and equip them for the most important task twelve men ever were asked to accomplish.

Modeling was a vital part of the teaching ministry of Christ:

And He went up to the mountain and summoned those whom He Himself wanted, and they came to Him. And He appointed twelve, that they might be with Him, and that He might send them out to preach (Mark 3:13-14).

Notice that an important part of the disciples' learning process was that they were *with* Him. While the Twelve learned from Christ's spoken instruction, the time they spent in His presence also was important. As they watched Jesus minister, they developed an awareness that went far beyond the actual words they heard. They came to love and follow their Master. And as that happened, their ministry skills developed too. Christ taught His apostles by *who* and *what* He was, as well as by what He said.

In chapter 2, we briefly mentioned the concept of discipling. Discipling is a form of teaching that extends its impact beyond actual instruction; which is to say, it is an educational approach that includes building a personal relationship with a learner. In the end, discipling's goal is to have a student incorporate his teacher's positive qualities into his own life. As Christ discipled

His followers, He explained the impact of true teaching:

> A pupil is not above his teacher; but everyone, after he has
> been fully trained, will be like his teacher (Luke 6:40).

This is precisely what happened in Christ's ministry. His
disciples lived with Him, learned from Him, and became like
Him. The character and commitment of Jesus had a transform-
ing effect on eleven of His twelve followers. And in the years
following His resurrection, this small group of disciples turned
the world upside down (Acts 17:6). We live and serve Christ
today because of the impact of their ministry and of those who
followed.

The Apostle Paul also discipled those whom he taught. He
addressed Timothy in a loving, fatherly manner:

> Timothy, my true child in the faith: Grace, mercy and peace
> from God the Father and Christ Jesus our Lord (1 Tim. 1:2).

As his words wonderfully reveal, it is clear that Paul felt a
deep concern for those whom he taught:

> Having thus a fond affection for you, we were well-pleased
> to impart to you not only the Gospel of God but also our
> own lives, because you had become very dear to us (1 Thes.
> 2:8).

Accordingly, Paul encouraged the believers at Philippi and
Corinth to model their lives after his example and after other
Christian teachers whom they had known:

> Brethren, join in following my example, and observe those
> who walk according to the pattern you have in us (Phil.
> 3:17).

Be imitators of me, just as I am also of Christ (1 Cor. 11:1).

It is important to recognize that biblical teaching involves more than transmitting content. Naturally, we must never demean the importance of the Scriptures' content; but the message of truth cannot be separated from the person who communicates that truth. The Bible is God's true and accurate revelation—whether or not it is taught, understood, or even read. But in order to teach its truths effectively, Scripture must be demonstrated and visualized through the life of the instructor. Such was the case in the ministry of Jesus Christ and in the teaching of Paul. This lesson *must* continue in our ministries today.

Spirit-guided Teaching

While in college, to help finance my studies, I took a number of jobs that required me to do direct sales work. Essentially, direct sales involves going up to the front door of a house, ringing the doorbell, and (hopefully) being invited in to show your product.

As you might well imagine, this whole procedure can be very intimidating for even a seasoned salesman, let alone an inexperienced rookie—such as I was. But in the companies I worked for, I soon found out that no rookie ever was sent out alone. We always were paired with an experienced salesman. We would watch and learn from him. Finally, when we had worked up our confidence, we'd try out the sales pitch on our own. However, the experienced salesman always was there to supervise our first few attempts. Ordinarily, he'd simply watch us without saying anything; but we knew he'd bail us out if we got in over our heads. That knowlege was very important to me. The mere *presence* of an expert salesman there to help out seemed encouraging. I had support. I was not alone.

The same is true in teaching. We are never alone.

As Christ was concluding His earthly ministry, He commanded His followers to make disciples of people all over the world:

> Go therefore and make disciples of all the nations, baptizing them in the name of the Father and the Son and the Holy Spirit, teaching them to observe all that I commanded you (Matt. 28:19-20).

When this command is stressed in missionary conferences today, an emphasis usually is placed on the word, "Go!" Unfortunately, few translations reflect the actual emphasis of this verse's Greek grammatical structure. If you were to read Matthew 28:19 in Greek, it would be very obvious that only one command is stressed—"Make disciples." Thus, a more accurate translation would read, "After you have gone, make disciples of all the nations."

This remains our mandate today—to help others become followers of Christ. In addition to being where Christ wants us to be ("Go therefore"), we also should be helping people get saved (as demonstrated through baptism), and then instructing them (teaching them to observe all things).

This is an awesome responsibility. Christ directs us to help others become followers of Him. But the most encouraging truth in those two verses is the final clause: "And lo, I am with you always, even to the end of the age." We have not been told to serve God alone.

A young boy asked his camp counselor how to teach a girl to swim. "Well," replied the counselor, "first you put your left arm around her waist. Then you take her right hand in your right. . . . "

"This girl is my sister," interrupted the camper.

"Oh, in that case, throw her out of the boat in the middle of the lake!'"

God is not like that. He doesn't throw us out of the boat and simply hope we can make it to shore. Rather, the continuing presence of Christ is a *fact* of our ministry experience. As you prepare to teach, He is with you. As you share information or lead discussions, He is there. As you guide learners in the exploration of truth, Jesus Christ is your constant companion—"even to the end of the age."

"But," you say, "I have never seen Him. And how can Christ be with me when He is seated at the right hand of the Father?" The same questions arose in the minds of the disciples as Christ was leaving the earth. They feared being alone. Jesus reassured them:

> But I tell you the truth, it is to your advantage that I go away; for if I do not go away, the Helper shall not come to you; but if I go, I will send Him to you (John 16:7).

While Christ did not personally remain with His disciples, He sent His Holy Spirit (the Helper) to stay with them; Christ's presence was in the Person of the Holy Spirit. The same Spirit indwells all believers today. This Spirit stands with us to encourage and comfort us. We are not left to our own wisdom and devices to serve God. This fact should make a great difference as we teach.

The Spirit's Promises

The Holy Spirit provides many gifts for believers. Consequently, it would be wise to consider two which are particularly important to us as teachers.

The first concerns the Spirit's promise to help us *understand truth*. Jesus told His disciples:

> I have many more things to say to you, but you cannot bear them now. But when He, the Spirit of Truth, comes, He

will guide you into all the truth (John 16:12-13).

Though Christ was an excellent communicator, His ability to teach His followers was subject to some limitations. This certainly was not due to His weakness as a teacher, but to the disciples' inability to receive information. They were not fully able to understand His message because the Holy Spirit had not yet come to indwell them. On the Day of Pentecost, the promised Holy Spirit came upon the early church. And since the establishment of the New Testament church, believers have received the Holy Spirit at the moment of their conversion.

Even today, as you study the Word in preparation for teaching, the Holy Spirit will help you understand spiritual truth:

Now we have received, not the spirit of the world, but the Spirit who is from God, that we might know the things freely given to us by God (1 Cor. 2:12).

It is God's Holy Spirit, given in fulfillment of Christ's promise, who remains with us. God's Spirit helps us understand spiritual truth so that we can serve Him effectively, so that we can contribute to making disciples of all the nations.

The second ministry of the Holy Spirit we will consider here involves the act of *convicting*. It is vital that teachers understand this ministry. Indeed, John writes that Christ Himself spoke of this particular function of the Holy Spirit:

And He, when He comes, will convict the world concerning sin, and righteousness, and judgment; concerning sin, because they do not believe in Me; and concerning righteousness, because I go to the Father, and you no longer behold Me; and concerning judgment, because the ruler of this world has been judged (John 16:8-11).

The concept of being convicted by the Holy Spirit often is misunderstood. Perhaps a better word to express this aspect of the Spirit's ministry would be "convincing." The Holy Spirit causes a person to become convinced of the truth of God's Word.

Quite often, when a person understands his sinful state before God, this understanding produces various emotional responses—such as being sorry for the sin and turning to God. But this is not always the case. Sorrow may or may not accompany conviction, and the person may or may not undergo change. The Holy Spirit does not force us to change against our will, but He *does* cause us to see the truth clearly. He convicts us of sin; that is, He convinces us that what God has said is true.

This means that as you are teaching, the Holy Spirit not only is working in you, but also is ministering to the learners— helping them to understand a given message. We pray that learners will respond to God. But this response is the decision of the learner. Neither the Holy Spirit nor the teacher is called to manipulate students into change.

Many teachers are greatly relieved when they realize they're not struggling alone to communicate God's message to students. It is a team effort. The Holy Spirit ministers both in the teacher and the learner. Teachers do not need to coax, plead, threaten, or otherwise intimidate learners. Rather, we need to guide students into an understanding and application of God's Word, knowing that Christ is with us in the Person of the Holy Spirit. Teachers must realize that God's Holy Spirit is working in the lives of the learners to convince them that the message is true and to call for an obedient response.

Application Activities

(1) How do you feel about the statement, "Teaching is an activity that promotes learning"? What impact do you think this

definition would have on your attitude toward teaching?

_____

_____

(2) How does it make you feel when you realize that those whom you teach will be learning as much (or more) from your life and character, as from the things you say in formal instruction?

_____

_____

(3) Write down several things which come to mind that will help you to build your Christian character so that it will reinforce the message you teach.

_____

_____

_____

_____

_____

_____

(4) Think of a time when the Holy Spirit convinced you or another person of a particular truth. Briefly describe what happened.

_____

_____

_____

_____

_____

_____

(5) What difference would it make if you, as a teacher, really were to understand and to be deeply impressed with the reality of the fact that the Holy Spirit works through your teaching?

_____

_____

_____

_____

CHAPTER FOUR
MOTIVATION AND LEARNING

You can gain a significant understanding of the teaching/learning process by observing what goes on in Sunday School classrooms. Some classes are models of decorum. Students sit quietly and politely with their chairs in even rows. There is a place for everything, and everything is in its place. The teacher obviously is in control. Students are doing just what they ought to be doing.

Other classrooms are quite the opposite. Students are moving around the room, noisily discussing things with one another. While everything may have its proper place, it appears as though it has been some time since supplies and equipment were stored in those places. Students, more than the teacher, seem to be in control of the class. Activity, commotion, and interaction are the rule, rather than peace, quiet, and independent activity.

We all know that such differences exist among Sunday School classes. But the real question is, which situation represents the more effective learning environment? I think most of us would agree that we feel more comfortable living in a slightly disheveled home—one that looks as though people actually reside in it—than in a demonstration model prepared by an interior decorator where everything is just right.

Similarly, I'm willing to argue that the most effective learning does *not* necessarily take place in a brightly polished, squeaky clean Sunday School classroom. If learning resources and accessories are to be used effectively, they cannot remain stored in neat, orderly boxes. Likewise, an effective learning environment can not be characterized by learners sitting quietly in rows. It also is terribly important to realize that keeping learners quiet often has nothing to do with actually teaching them.

Instead, exuberance and activity should be the hallmarks of true learning. Some of the best learning takes place when students interact with one another and with the teacher. When people are excited about learning, when they are gaining new insights, they may find it impossible to sit quietly and peacefully.

Stimulating Internal Motivation

A classroom characterized by discovery and growth rarely will be calm and peaceful—but learning *will* take place. Why? Because learners are highly motivated. True motivation must come from *within* a student; it represents his or her internal drive or desire to accomplish something. Therefore, a wise teacher will look for ways to stimulate that internal motivation. This desire to ignite inner motivation characterizes effective, life-changing teaching.

Unfortunately, many people think that keeping order, or making sure that learners remain quiet, is the most important part of teaching. It *is* true that students need to pay attention to a given lesson and not participate in disruptive activities if they are to learn. If students are running around, screaming their heads off, no one in the classroom will be able to learn easily. But rather than demanding order, it is better for teachers to teach in such a way that students, themselves, are motivated to learn. When this happens, students will *want* to pay attention. Instead of the teacher trying to figure out strategies to keep attention focused, learners themselves become accountable.

Certain techniques can manipulate students into behaving without actually stimulating their internal motivation to learn. Most of these devices, though, are short-lived and of minimal value. For instance, if you offered a monetary reward to everyone who passed an exam on a certain lesson, most students probably would be willing to learn that information. But if the offer were withdrawn, learning probably would cease too. Likewise, you might threaten a learner with punishment if he fails to master a lesson. As long as that person is intimidated, he may, to some extent, learn. But you can be sure that no great love for learning will develop in his life. And as soon as your threats cease, whatever learning *did* take place will cease as well.

The actions of one enterprising young girl exemplify the inadequacy of depending on external motivation to get learners to participate. The Sunday School she went to sponsored an attendance contest. Each student was promised a dollar for every visitor he or she brought to class. This girl set the record for bringing the most visitors. A quick investigation, though, revealed how she had managed to lure her twenty visitors: she simply paid each one fifty cents out of the dollar she earned. She had recognized a good business deal and took advantage of it. Her motivation, then, was purely external and lasted only until the contest ended.

True motivation is internal, and a primary goal of teaching is to stimulate that motivation in learners. Only when this occurs will students want to pay attention and continue to learn. We will not have to buy their participation or bribe them into cooperation. Accordingly, this chapter introduces a number of effective teaching strategies to develop internal motivation. Specifically, I will suggest three different approaches to triggering internal motivation. Teachers can encourage their students to learn through providing answers to *felt needs*, arousing *interest* in learners, or providing opportunities for *dynamic interaction*.

Need Motivation

The easiest type of motivation for a teacher to use is *need motivation*. It is easy to employ because the learner comes to the teacher ready to learn. The student knows that he has a particular need and is looking for help in meeting it. He has a spiritual hunger and is looking for someone who can show him how to satisfy it.

Let's look at an example of need motivation in another field. Assume you're teaching a class on first-aid techniques. Today's lesson deals with CPR (cardio-pulmonary resuscitation). Just as your class members are entering the building, one of them has a heart attack. In desperation, one person is dispatched to call for assistance while fellow class members frantically await the arrival of the emergency squad. When the paramedics arrive, they do all they can to save the victim's life. But it is too late. In sorrow and frustration the paramedics turn to the crowd. "Why didn't anyone here administer CPR?" they ask. "If any of you had known CPR and had helped this person, he probably would be alive right now."

Imagine now that your class members enter the room and tell you all that has happened. In light of this recent experience, you'd find it relatively easy to motivate them to learn CPR techniques. In light of their experience, they are highly motivated by a felt need. All you have to do is respond to that need.

Notice that the *needs* of these class members have not changed; they've needed to learn CPR all along. Only now, they've developed a heightened awareness of their need. In educational terms, a *real* need has become a *felt* need. That is, the learners themselves know their need and are looking for help in resolving it.

If Sunday School teachers always had students with *felt* needs, teaching would be amazingly simple. But that rarely is the case. As a result, the teacher must look for other ways to trigger internal motivation. That means helping learners identify their needs and making those desires *felt* needs. So how can that be done?

Many teachers are unaware of the importance which the introduction portion of a Sunday School lesson plays. Yet the main purpose of an introduction is to help learners become aware of their real needs. If in introducing a lesson, you can share an anecdote, a personal illustration, or a hypothetical situation that stimulates need motivation, learners will be more inclined to participate in the learning process. They eventually may begin to feel those needs that you, the teacher, suspect are actual needs in their lives.

Of course, this is not to imply that we know every need a learner has. Only God knows that. But teachers can understand and address their teaching to meet those needs that God has revealed. For example, all people need to know Christ as Saviour. We all must grow toward increased spiritual maturity. And we need to build relationships within the body of Christ and look for ways to minister to others.

Other needs correlate with personal growth or specific situations that individuals face. As children grow, they have basic needs that correspond to their age and maturity. But these basic needs vary somewhat from child to child. Good teachers recognize where specific children are in their maturity and consequent needs. Thus, the better a teacher knows a learner, the more he or she will become aware of that student's specific problems and personal needs.

We will consider the importance of lesson introductions in more detail as we examine how to put together a lesson plan. For now, I simply would like you to realize that anything you legitimately can do to help learners recognize their real needs will arouse internal motivation. Since we cannot always count on learners being sensitive to their own needs, we must be prepared to stimulate that awareness.

Interest Motivation

Another way to stimulate a learner's motivation is through a technique known as *interest motivation*. This refers to the use of varied and effective teaching methods to make instruction interesting and attractive to learners. When a person is doing something that he really enjoys or that is highly interesting to him, no coaxing is necessary to encourage continued participation.

Some people work far harder at their hobbies than they do at the jobs where they earn their living. No one *makes* these individuals work at their hobbies; certain activities simply are interesting and satisfying for them. For those reasons alone, they'll give great attention to their leisure time pursuits. No one has to remind a person who loves to read good mysteries that he should pay attention to the book. Because he is interested, he will give it his undivided attention. No one has to tell a football fan to pay attention when his favorite team is playing for the national championship. If he is a true fan, you probably couldn't drag him away from the game with a tow truck. When you teach a Sunday School class in an interesting manner, using attractive methods, learners will pay attention too.

We've all observed boring classes. Sometimes the teacher appears more bored than anyone else. The story is told of an absent-minded professor who dreamed he was lecturing. He woke up and found that he was! Now that's boring! If a teacher is disinterested in the subject being taught, the rest of the class probably will be bored to tears as well. Yet when a teacher is excited, and communicates a high level of interest in his presentation, there is a much better chance that learners will be highly motivated. This is due to the fact that the more interested a teacher is in the subject matter being shared, the more a learner will pay attention to it.

One way to help make your presentation interesting is to include illustrations that have high interest value. If, for example, you're discussing a Christian's obligation to help the poor, use a strong anecdote to drive this truth home. Find a story about a woman who's opened her home to refugees, or a man who spends every weekend volunteering in a shelter for dispossessed persons. Such illustrations could be found in a newspaper or magazine. They could be personal anecdotes from your own life. Or they could come from a wide variety of other sources. Whatever the source, it's of utmost importance that your illustration be interesting to the learners and relevant to the concept being communicated. The more interesting your anecdotes are, the more effectively they will trigger interest motivation.

A second way to stimulate interest is to use humor effectively. Some teachers can tell good jokes—and even make them sound funny. Others can tell stories well or relate humorous anecdotes. When learners enjoy themselves, they tend to be more interested in the subject than when they are bored and unhappy. So recognize the funny or enjoyable things that happen in class. If a class member makes a humorous comment, enjoy it with the rest of the class. Take advantage of these situations to liven up a class session and help build good relationships with the learners. One word of caution about humor, though. It is always inappropriate to use sarcastic or unkind humor. Demeaning class members or joking at their expense should never be encouraged. Whenever you employ humor, make it fun and enjoyable, never cutting or humiliating.

A third—and one of the best ways to trigger motivation through interest—is through the use of multisensory communication. Teachers who primarily lecture assume students only use the sense of hearing. Unfortunately, relying exclusively on hearing is unwise. It has been estimated that the average person can process information four times faster than a teacher can speak. If this is true, it means that listeners are seriously underchallenged. And if they're not being challenged, they're probably being bored.

Since we have five senses, why limit our Sunday School teaching to only one? The obvious answer is, we shouldn't! The more senses we employ, the more interesting—and, consequently, the more effective—our teaching will be. Thus, anytime we help learners visualize ideas, we increase our teaching effectiveness. Objects to feel, smell, taste, and look at—such as food, perfume, artifacts, pictures, charts, diagrams, or chalkboard illustrations—should be used. The secret is to communicate through as many of the five senses as possible. Using more channels of communication (senses) will make our teaching more interesting.

Dynamic Interaction

As we've seen, expecting learners to come to class already interested in the lesson is somewhat naive. While students may be highly motivated some of the time, the teacher who routinely expects such excitement will be sorely disappointed. We should rejoice when learners come with high interest, but we ought not be surprised when they don't.

We've also determined that instructional methods which make use of illustrations, humor, and a variety of senses can significantly improve a learner's motivation. But the technique that might prove most effective in this regard is that which includes elements of *dynamic interaction*—that is, techniques that get learners *working together*. Because these techniques depend on the dynamics of group interaction, they can draw in students who might otherwise be reluctant to participate. As a result, they substantially increase the effectiveness of the Sunday School lesson.

One reason dynamic motivation is so effective is that learners are encouraged to interact with each other. Do you remember the hypothetical classrooms that we considered at the beginning of this chapter? When learners are free to interact with one another and the atmosphere is relaxed, greater learning can occur. Few people learn well in isolation. But when they are interacting in a cooperative learning endeavor, they will learn more and will retain much more of what they learn.

Another reason dynamic interaction is so effective is that learning takes on more meaning when relationships are growing. As the teacher builds relationships with learners, and learners relate to each other, respect and appreciation develop. And where mutual respect exists, learning increases.

One study evaluated the impact of lectures, multisensory instruction, and dynamic interaction. The researchers found that when a variety of senses are used in the learning process, up to five times as much information can be communicated than when lecture alone is used. But even more dramatic results were obtained with interactive methods. When learners were encouraged to work interactively, ten times as much learning occurred as when the teacher merely talked. This study showed, therefore, that interactive teaching doubles even the highly effective yield of the multisensory approach. When students interact and build relationships, learning is maximized.

A third reason for using dynamic methods involves the fact that they teach life skills in addition to communicating truth. All of us need to learn to work with others. At work, in our homes, and especially as believers, we must share cooperatively. We are called on to build up and encourage each other.

The better we do this, the more effectively we can serve at work, at home, and in the church. Dynamic methods not only increase Church School teaching effectiveness, but help learners interact and build relationships they can use to reach out and minister to others in need.

In a later chapter, we'll fully examine how to use dynamic methods in teaching. We'll look at how to employ techniques such as group discussion, problem solving, and question-and-answer sessions. When teachers use these methods, they can draw learners more completely into the teaching/ learning process. Sunday School classes will no longer be a time when a frustrated teacher arrives with a mass of information to be dumped on disinterested learners. Instead, learners will become responsible, active participants. They will not be able to sit on the sidelines as passive observers. Both teachers *and* learners will come to enjoy the educational process.

Application Activities

(1) Why do many people seem to feel that the greatest amount of learning takes place in the quietest classroom?

_____

_____

_____

(2) Think back to one time when you really wanted to learn something. Why do you think you were so interested, and what part did another person play in your interest?

_____

_____

_____

(3) Recall a time when you or someone you know was motivated by a felt need. Briefly describe the situation and explain what you or that other person did to have that need met.

_____

_____

_____

_____

_____

_____

_____

(4) Make a list of sources you could turn to for illustrations and anecdotes to make your teaching more interesting.

_____

_____

_____

_____

_____

_____

_____

_____

(5) Describe your effectiveness in telling jokes or including spontaneous humor in conversation. Do you think that humor would be good for you to use in teaching?

_____

_____

_____

(6) Why do you think some teachers are fearful of allowing group discussion in their classes, and how do you think that fear can be conquered?

_____

_____

_____

_____

CHAPTER FIVE
WORDS AND BEYOND

Please read the following statement: "I love you." What do those words mean to you? Out of context, they hold very little meaning. Yet all of us know how terribly significant this phrase is when it's addressed to someone we cherish. The words in this sentence are simply a combination of letters—like all other words. But the commitment and feelings which they transmit can be life-transforming. At this point, they no longer are mere words. They now become communication.

Because an adequate understanding of communication is crucial to effective Sunday School teaching, we would do well to spend some time examining this key factor.

Elements of Effective Communication

As we've just seen, communication involves more than merely stringing together series of words. In actuality, several dimensions of effective communication can readily be identified:

(1) _Vocal Inflection._ If you could hear me say the words, "I love you" out loud, a whole new element would be added to

them. The inflection of my voice, the emphasis I place on certain words over others, and the emotion I feel as I speak them all would be relevant factors in communicating that sentence. And, depending on the context in which I say those words, my vocal inflection could significantly influence the meaning my listener attaches to this message.

I am writing these words as I sit in a hotel in New Orleans. This morning, I said good-bye to my wife before leaving to come here on a short business trip. As I walked out the door, I told Elaine that I loved her. As I spoke those words, there was a trace of sadness and regret in my voice. I already knew that I was going to miss her, and I felt sad. I wanted to assure Elaine that I loved her even though I would not be there to tell her so. My vocal inflection probably conveyed that sentiment.

Now suppose I have just returned from my trip. When we greet each other at the airport and throw our arms around one another, I'll again say, "I love you." But now my vocal inflection will reflect the joy I feel at being reunited with my wife.

In teaching, our vocal inflection also assumes an important role. If we proclaim, "Jesus is Lord," yet our voice conveys that fact in a dull, listless tone, our students will have heard *words*. They will not have gained a true appreciation of the significance of this message. We must constantly be aware that teaching is not just a matter of *what* we say, but *how* we say it.

(2) *Individualized Word Meaning.* The words we use are symbols; we select them to represent objects and ideas. All of us, however, bring private connotations to the words we hear and use. While we must recognize this fact in everyday communication, it is even more important to take notice of this phenomenon in our teaching. Because we bring our own personal experiences and interpretations to the words we use, even frequently used terms don't mean exactly the same thing to any two persons.

Suppose I say that God is like a father. This is a true statement—*if* we have an accurate perception of a father's proper role and understand how he should act. God *is* like a father. But what if I tell that to a child whose father comes home drunk and beats her? God certainly is not similar to *that* kind of father. As you can see, we may not communicate the intended truth to our listener because of the dissimilar ways people interpret the same word. So in addition to recognizing the significance and impact of vocal inflection, we must recognize that an individual's personalized definition of words makes verbal communication difficult.

(3) *Body Language.* Whenever we communicate, we convey more than our words or the sound of those words and phrases. Body language is one term that has been used to express a form of *unspoken* communication.

Observe two people engaged in conversation. Usually, they use gestures, posture, and a variety of other physical techniques to reinforce and interpret their words. Teachers also employ body language, though many are unaware that they do.

Often, by noticing a Sunday School teacher's demeanor at the beginning of class, one can get a fairly good idea of whether he is happy to be there. The posture and position he takes while teaching is part of his body language. A teacher who is seated in a circle with his students is indicating a desire to share and discuss ideas with them. In contrast, a teacher who stands behind a lectern, firmly grasping the top, lecturing to students seated in formal rows, may be communicating something entirely different. He probably will be perceived as someone who wants to retain control. He is likely to generate far less discussion and participation among his students than the seated teacher.

To sum up, the way in which a teacher communicates in the classroom will significantly influence the outcome of the teaching/learning experience. Through skillful use of inflection and careful word choices, as well as body language, wise teachers modify and expand on the words they use to promote learning. (Incidentally, because I recognize these facts, when I greet my wife at the airport upon returning from this trip, I will reinforce the words "I love you" with body language: I'll give Elaine a big hug and a kiss!)

Excellent teachers do not rely solely on words to communicate with learners. As we noticed in the last chapter, they incorporate a *variety* of techniques to reinforce and support those words. These techniques take advantage of senses other than that of hearing. Skillful teachers recognize that God has provided us with five senses, and they take advantage of as many of them as possible.

Teaching through Five Senses

One of the activities that I enjoy for relaxation (and nourishment) is gardening. It's exciting and gratifying to prepare the soil, plant the seeds, care for the tender seedlings, and nurture the maturing plants. But then comes the best part of all—harvesting and eating the fresh, delicious vegetables.

Gardening involves a great deal of work, and any number of pitfalls can snag a budding gardener. We must deal with countless forces conspiring against us: bugs, drought, wind, and raccoons—to name a few. Fortunately, there are good resources available to amateurs such as I. Gardening books, for example, can explain what trouble spots to watch out for, and can show me how to counteract the little rascals that frustrate my horticultural efforts.

But the best instructions in the world are useless if I choose to ignore them. For instance, since we live in northern Illinois, my planting must be done in the latter part of spring—otherwise, a late frost could play havoc with sprouting seeds. Of course, I *could* plant my seeds anytime I wished, and then simply pray for a fruitful harvest. But planting seeds in the fall and asking God to bless such efforts would be contradictory. If I am to expect God's blessing on my efforts, I need to work in cooperation with the laws of nature He has created.

This means I must do all I can to understand God's laws of agriculture. Then I must plan my garden and implement those plans in accordance with the principles that govern those activities. Whether I am a Christian or not, God's natural laws operate. A non-Christian who knows and follows God's natural laws will reap a better harvest than a Christian who knows them but chooses to disregard them.

Sunday School teaching has much in common with gardening. Just as natural laws govern agriculture, so certain laws apply to communication. The good teacher is one who knows and functions within the limitations of those laws. If we teach only through the sense of hearing, we will be far less effective than those teachers who use methods which employ the other four senses.

Much time has been spent in recent years studying human communication. It has become abundantly clear that limiting ourselves to words alone—even with the helpful aid of verbal inflection and appropriate body language—greatly hinders effective communication.

Numerous studies also have confirmed that we retain no more than 10 percent of what we hear. This finding means that if a Sunday School teacher limits himself to a lecture format, his students will—at a maximum—remember only one tenth of the material presented.

A friend of mine told me of a teacher for whom he once worked. This man spoke to a class faster than anyone else my friend had ever heard. But outside of class, this same teacher spoke at a very normal speed. When my friend asked him why he lectured so quickly in class, the teacher replied that he had heard that students retain only 10 percent of all they hear. He figured that if he simply talked faster, and crammed in more information, they would remember more.

Unfortunately, this teacher's reasoning contained a critical fallacy. He failed to realize that a person manages to retain one tenth of what he hears only under *optimal* conditions. When a speaker is boring, the subject uninteresting, or if learners have negative attitudes, this percentage declines dramatically. Thus, speaking quickly will not improve a listener's ability to retain information. Potentially, it could aggravate a learner and actually *decrease* his retention rate.

These findings hold several important implications. For one, teachers who really desire to communicate well will not limit themselves to words alone—even interesting ones. They will look for other ways to increase the effectiveness of their communication. The study which confirmed that we retain about 10 percent of what we hear also reported the results of visual-oriented communication. It concluded that when we substitute visual techniques for verbal ones, a learner can retain *twice* as much information. And when the two—verbal and visual methods—are combined, the increase over verbal communication alone was fivefold.

In short, if we use visual methods alone, learners may remember a maximum of 10 percent of what we share. But when we use methods that combine the senses of sight and hearing, those same learners could retain 50 percent, or one half, of what was shared. This represents a good stewardship of our time and talents. Since we are concerned with teaching God's truths as effectively as possible, it only makes sense to look for and employ those methods which will help us accomplish the job.

Imagine for a minute that my garden is very dry. I begin to water it, but I only use one garden hose. You notice that there are five faucets on the back of my house (there aren't, but humor me) and I have five garden hoses coiled by those faucets. As I complain to you about how long it takes to water my garden, you become increasingly puzzled. Finally you ask me why I don't use all five hoses. "It's too much work to connect the other four hoses," I reply. So I continue watering slowly and gripe about how inefficient this method is. But that type of attitude is foolish. If I *really* were concerned about getting the job done, I would use all the tools at my disposal.

The five hoses, obviously, represent the five senses we can use for communication purposes. In addition to hearing, we also can employ sight, touch, taste, and smell. This is not to say that all five should be used all the time. But we should make use of those that are appropriate to a given lesson. And remember: the more we use, the greater our potential for effective communication will be. Unfortunately, many teachers never bother to "connect" the other four hoses and attempt to accomplish the Sunday School teaching task with severely limited resources. God has given us multiple channels for communication. Let's use them to His glory.

Resources You Can Use

Many teachers know how important it is to use all five senses in the classroom. Yet they often fail to take advantage of the resources available to help them involve learners in this way.

Recently, Scripture Press conducted a nationwide study of Sunday School teachers. These teachers taught young people in a wide variety of denominational and independent churches across America. Most were using well-designed curriculum materials to guide them in teaching their classes. The report indicated, however, that barely half of these teachers were using the multisensory teaching aid resources designed by the publishers of those materials.

Any teacher striving to teach effectively *should* consider using such teaching resources. If the publisher does not offer good resources, then alternative materials should be examined. The rationale for purchasing such curriculum is that professionals have designed those resources to promote effective teaching.

Resources have been planned and compiled that the average teacher would have difficulty securing for himself. Using these multisensory materials, he can teach far more effectively than if he were left to his own preparation.

After consulting the prepared publisher's resources, a good next step is to consider additional teaching techniques suggested in the curriculum materials. All materials should offer suggestions concerning specific methods which can be used to increase teaching effectiveness. Usually these are included right in the body of the lesson. They essentially walk you through the activities to be used in teaching that lesson.

According to the same survey mentioned above, most teachers of young people *do* have resources available for use in teaching. The following chart is excerpted from that study and shows the percentage of teachers who have equipment available, and the percentage of those church school instructors having equipment available who actually used it in the previous three months.

Equipment	Available to Use	Actually Used
Chalkboard	95.4	54.2
Filmstrip Projector	70.8	24.9
Movie Projector	70.3	37.8
Record Player	68.6	24.4
Cassette Recorder/Player	68.0	49.4
Overhead Projector	68.0	39.7
Slide Projector	57.5	25.7
Video Recorder/Player	13.9	40.2

It's hard to believe that only half of these teachers had used a chalkboard in the last several months—even though more than 95 percent of those teachers had one available! In some cases, perhaps teachers weren't sure of the best way to use resources such as a chalkboard. But for others, it clearly indicates a lack of awareness of how important such resources can be in stimulating involvement through a variety of senses.

An element of laziness or procrastination also may be evident here. Some teachers feel that preparing to use such equipment takes too much time. Or, if they are preparing their lesson on Saturday night (or worse yet, on Sunday morning), they are desperate to figure out what to say. As a result, they never even get around to considering whether they might be able to use more effective teaching methods.

It is beyond the scope of this brief chapter to explain the use of audiovisual methods in detail. Hopefully, teachers will recognize the value of such methods and will follow the suggestions found in their curriculum materials. Or, if they're not using prepared curriculum materials, they should evaluate published materials and select the best available resources.

As an example, though, let's consider some ways that the chalkboard can be used to improve teaching. While these suggestions are by no means exhaustive, they are methods that I personally have used in my teaching. Most of them have been used with fourth-grade and older learners, though some could be used with younger age-groups.

Before Class Begins
—Write a thought provoking question.
—Write a summary statement from the previous week.
—Write an agree/disagree statement. (You can begin class by discussing their opinions.)
—Draw a chart or diagram that you will refer to in class.
—List your goals for the class session. (You do have some, don't you?)
—Write a "wrong" statement that you ask your students to evaluate and/or correct.

During the Class Session
—Use a diagram to show the relationship of ideas.
—Use stick figures to show relationships between people. (Don't worry about being an artist; if they look funny, that's even better.)
—List the outline of the class session.
—List ideas and suggestions that come from class members.
—List solutions to problems you are discussing in class.
—List subjects that need further study.
—List questions you are seeking to answer from the Bible.

At the End of Class
—Write decisions students might have suggested or made.
—List application ideas.
—Write down assignments for the coming week.
—Write the dates of coming activities.
—List answers to questions or conclusions that were drawn.
—List expected behaviors based on the lessons learned.

Many other possible applications also exist. A teacher never should neglect using a chalkboard, even for one week, let alone three months (though I admit keeping a supply of chalk in your classroom can be quite a challenge). It is a valuable resource tool and should be used. If no chalkboard is available, use a flip chart or sheets of newsprint taped to the wall (newsprint is the paper on which newspapers are printed; it usually can be purchased from your local newspaper publisher). Use masking tape; it will not remove paint as cellophane tape will. Write on the newsprint with a felt-tip marker or with crayon.

We could discuss each of the other seven methods listed in the chart above, but that is beyond our present purposes. You can refer to your teacher's guide for specific suggestions, or purchase an inexpensive booklet which describes how to use these methods from your local bookstore.

At first you may feel somewhat uncomfortable trying out a new method. But a simple three-point outline will help you master any one of them. The points are as follows: (1) Practice, (2) Practice, (3) Practice.

I once observed an excellent teacher effectively using his chalkboard. Naturally, I wondered how he had developed such skill. In response to my question, he told me that before each session, he went into the classroom alone and *practiced* writing every single thing he planned to put on the board.

Is it any wonder that he was so skillful? He was dedicated to doing an excellent job. And he was willing to go that extra mile because he thought the spiritual destiny of his students was worth the effort. Do you agree with him? Is it worth some time and effort to improve the quality of your teaching?

Remember our gardening illustration and the value of connecting more than one hose. God has given us five effective channels of communication. Since the content of biblical teaching is truly important, we dare not ignore four of those channels.

And while you are developing skills in trying new teaching methods, don't ever forget the three-point outline for effectiveness. Remember to PRACTICE, PRACTICE, PRACTICE!

Application Activities

(1) Describe the various ways in which a public communicator such as Billy Graham uses body language to increase his effectiveness.

_____

_____

_____

(2) Do you think you would feel more comfortable teaching

from a standing or a seated position? Why do you feel that way? Could your feelings be different under various circumstances?

_____

_____

(3) Why do so many teachers have a tendency to resort to lecturing, rather than using other, more interesting and effective methods?

_____

_____

(4) Describe a teaching experience where you observed someone using a methodology that did not rely entirely on spoken communication.

_____

_____

(5) Why do you think only about half of the teachers in the survey used the chalkboard when it was available?

_____

_____

_____

(6) Of the eight equipment resources listed on the chart in this chapter, which are available to you? Which ones have you ever attempted to use in teaching? Which do you think you could use most effectively?

_____

_____

_____

For guidance on planning and using multisensory teaching methods consult: Kenneth Gangel, *Twenty-four Ways to Improve Your Teaching* (Victor Books), or *Teaching Techniques for Church Education* (Evangelical Teacher Training Association).

CHAPTER SIX
TEACHING THROUGH INVOLVEMENT

No one seems to be quite sure how and when it happens, but it does happen. Some people believe that students are born that way, but teachers know they're not. Others think Sunday School causes it, but it's a problem that exists in other places as well. Some teachers think it happens only in their classes, but that merely indicates they haven't seen what transpires in other classrooms. Whenever and however it happens, we know that it does occur.

What I'm referring to, of course, is the point at which students get the idea that learning is a passive activity. At some point in a person's education, he or she stops participating in class and just sits there. And we wonder what causes it. Some educators suggest that we teachers, and our teaching methods, may be a contributing factor.

But why speculate? Why not just find out for yourself? Take a tour through your Sunday School and discover what is going on. It may help you gain some insights into this problem.

Look at the Nursery class. What are children doing there?

They may enthusiastically be singing "Jesus Loves Me," or doing finger plays, or "listening" to a Bible story by giving the teacher frequent and insistent suggestions as to how it should be told.

Look at the four- and five-year-olds. What are they doing? Singing, or doing handcraft, or acting out a Bible story? Perhaps they have put their chairs in a row and are "riding a bus" to Sunday School. Whatever they're doing, you can be sure that it's *active*. They are involved and enthusiastic. They're exhibiting an exuberance that can leave you breathless.

Drop in on the Primaries. They too will be active. Some may be asking questions. And others, bursting with excitement, will frantically wave their hands to be called on. They also may be doing handcrafts to help them understand biblical truths. Or they may be working out of their student manuals. But they won't be passive—and they rarely are quiet.

Now look at the Junior Highs. A very different situation appears here. These students often sit staring glumly at the teacher—or off into space. If the teacher attempts to ask them a question, there's a good possibility he'll have to answer it himself. Faced with such indifference, the teacher may have resorted to a straight lecture format—grinding it out week after week, perpetuating the cycle of boredom. Many times, the High School class is no better. The students sleepily follow the pattern of the younger teen class.

The same problem continues in the adult classes. We aren't sure why, but most adults seem to prefer passive learning. Perhaps it is because many adult teachers seem to feel their primary purpose is simply to dispense that information. One application a week, with the dosage dictated by the length of time remaining after the "preliminaries" are over. Once the juice and donuts are put away, praise and prayer notes shared, birthdays and anniversaries in the coming week remembered, missionaries prayed for, attendance and offering taken, the next social planned, and miscellaneous announcements made, the teacher is allotted a token amount of time to "give the lesson."

And give it he does. Since there's so little time, and since he has so much information to transmit, all the teacher can imagine doing is lecturing, perhaps at top speed. "The lesson" stands out in marked contrast to the rest of the session. Usually, class interaction and participation is at its greatest level during the "preliminaries." But when the teacher stands up, the students' involvement in the class comes screeching to a stop.

Why Get Students Involved?

What has happened? Think back to the preschool and early elementary classes. What did we observe? A great deal of student interaction occurred, didn't it? The learners were involved, active, participating. But this important element in the teaching/learning process seems to have been forgotten when we got to the teen years and beyond. Apparently, someone decided that youth and adults learn passively; learners serve as receivers, teachers act as transmitters.

You may have noticed something else in the younger departments. Most of the teachers probably were telling the children to be quiet. Now this tactic doesn't work with preschoolers. And Primaries usually don't respond to such instructions any better. But after years of being told to keep quiet in class, by the time learners reach the teen years, the message seems to have sunk in.

Is it any wonder, then, that teen and adult learners tend to be passive? They often prefer to sit back and see what the teacher has to offer—what kind of a lesson he has prepared, and how well he delivers it. This doesn't happen as often in the younger classes. Few teachers try to teach younger children without actually *involving* them, because children don't respond well in a passive environment. Children still think that learning should be active, and that they ought to be involved.

Consequently, rather than trying to stifle our students' desires to interact in class, teachers need to channel it. Fortunately, there are numerous ways to nurture and secure such involvement.

First, we can teach in a way that meets the felt needs of our students (see chapter 4). However, teachers cannot rely exclusively on this technique because we do not always know our learners' needs. Likewise, learners sometimes arrive in Sunday School with little overt interest in the lesson topic, even though they need to learn it.

Therefore, we also need to encourage involvement through sensory communication. Do you remember the advantages of this approach that we considered in the last chapter? If more of the learner's senses are involved in the educational process, our communication will be more effective. And, if while employing various senses, we communicate in an interesting manner, even more material will be understood.

But we need not be satisfied with these levels of communication; a third type of involvement further increases our effectiveness. It's a method which depends on the mechanics of group interaction to draw learners into the teaching/learning process. It is interesting, effective, and has a high potential for leading to life-changing learning. As I mentioned in chapter 4, this method is known as *dynamic interaction*. Now seems a good time to explore this concept in greater detail.

Relationships and Dynamic Interaction

It is safe to assume that Jesus was an excellent teacher. He not only possessed an infinite knowledge of all subjects, but He totally knew the people whom He taught. The methods that He used also were the best possible. He spoke to His followers' needs, and He did it interestingly. Our Lord used a variety of senses and communicated effectively.

But His deepest teaching was done among those with whom

He had cultivated personal relationships. The call to be a fol-
lower of Christ implied a mandate to future ministry. But beyond that, it demonstrated that Jesus was willing and eager to
build personal relationships with those who responded to His
call.

> And He appointed twelve, that they might be with Him, and
> that He might send them out to preach, and to have author-
> ity to cast out the demons (Mark 3:14-15).

Christ's disciples were called to learn from Him and then
minister to others. Christ was their example as He ministered to
people wherever He went. But before the disciples were sent
out, they needed to get to know Christ personally, as well as the
truth of His instructions. Thus, Jesus made use of dynamic
interaction.

Apparently, this technique worked well, for near the end of
His ministry, Jesus commented on the extent to which His
disciples should have been influenced through their personal
interaction with Him:

> Jesus said to him, "Have I been so long with you, and yet
> you have not come to know Me, Philip? He who has seen
> Me has seen the Father; how do you say, 'Show us the
> Father'?" (John 14:9)

Because the nature of true teaching involves building personal relationships, Jesus explained that when a person is fully
trained (or discipled), he will be like his teacher (Luke 6:40).

It's a truth worth repeating: Learning is best accomplished
when a high level of interaction and communication exists
between teacher and learner. For this reason, we must plan and
implement teaching methods that bring learners into contact
with each other, as well as with their teacher.

Teaching must be more than making a presentation to a group of learners. Ideally, it involves cultivating an environment where interactive learning can take place. And when this environment has been provided, the teacher can guide learners through the teaching/learning process. Life-changing learning often will be the result.

But even a good teacher must consciously plan the use of dynamic involvement. When teaching younger age-groups, teachers may find that learners want *too much* interaction. Sometimes younger learners create a problem by wanting to interact about everything *except* the lesson. In that case, the teacher should devise strategies that channel interaction. Channeling the desire for interaction is much better than trying to suppress it.

On the other hand, the problem with most groups of older learners is one of getting them to participate *at all*. Because they have acquired passive learning habits, the teacher has to plan methods to draw them out, get them involved, and stimulate productive interaction. The following suggested methods are designed to accomplish both of these goals: to channel interaction and to draw out reluctant learners.

Question/Answer. A very effective way to draw students into the learning process is through the effective use of questions. Questions can fall into two categories: those which learners direct to the teacher or to other learners, and those which the teacher asks. Both types of queries contribute significantly to effective learning.

Some teachers seem to feel that if their students ask them questions, this indicates they've done a poor job of teaching. Actually, the converse is true. Excellent teachers don't merely pour out every bit of information they've acquired. Rather, they teach in a thought-provoking way which stimulates learners to ask questions.

The teaching of Christ abounds with this technique. Many

of His parables were designed specifically to elicit questions from His listeners. And He succeeded. After hearing the parables about the true nature of the kingdom of God, Christ's disciples had questions.

> Then He left the multitudes, and went into the house. And His disciples came to Him saying, "Explain to us the Parable of the Tares in the Field" (Matt. 13:36).

Christ did just that. He answered their questions, and in so doing, provided them with a level of understanding which surpassed the knowledge they would have obtained had He simply lectured. Because their curiosity and interest were aroused, the disciples became deeply involved in the teaching/learning process.

Good teachers also plan to ask *good* questions to evoke responses from learners. Notice the emphasis on the word good. Some types of questions do not actually promote interaction. Questions with yes/no answers, or those which require a simple factual response, are of limited value. Yet when good instructional questions are asked, students will be challenged to wrestle with the implications of the material. To secure interaction, you need to ask "why?" or "what do you think?" kinds of questions. These indicate to the learner that his input is a vital and significant part of the learning experience.

Finally, when legitimate differences of opinion crop up among those in your class, don't become alarmed. One excellent way for students to understand their feelings and beliefs is to discuss them verbally with those who hold differing views. Recognize that an important goal of Sunday School teaching is the establishment of dynamic relationships among learners; you're not necessarily trying to find definitive answers to the great theological issues of our day and age.

Discussion. A group discussion is more than people randomly speaking out on a subject. The best way to describe a good discussion, I believe, is to consider it a cooperative search for an acceptable solution to a mutually agreed-upon problem.

Notice that this definition contains several elements. First, it assumes the existence of an agreed-upon problem. Groups rarely will discusss a matter unless they feel a real problem needs to be solved. For this reason, a good teacher ordinarily will take time to provide learners with background information on the problem and establish the importance of the topic.

Let's assume you've been asked to lead an adult Sunday School class. One "problem" you might deal with in your class is how parents and teenagers can communicate more effectively. You explain the various barriers to communication which exist between parents and teens: different tastes in clothes, music, and leisure-time pursuits.

Having thus defined the problem area to be discussed, the group then should cooperatively interact as they seek to find constructive solutions. Usually, this process will entail three phases. In the first phase the group will clarify and come to an understanding of the problem. The second phase is to suggest as many solutions to the problem as possible. The final phase involves selecting the best solution (or perhaps combination of solutions) to that problem. Perhaps you'll decide that, as parents, you'll listen to your teens' favorite albums, and then discuss your reactions to this music with them. In this way, you'll be opening up parent/teenager lines of communication.

An acceptable solution is, by definition, one with which all members are comfortable. It will not always be the ideal solution, but it must be one which both resolves the difficulty and is acceptable to all class members.

A note of caution: in discussion situations, the teacher must never imply that when the discussion is completed, he will give the "correct" answer to the problem being considered. If he does, then learners will feel manipulated and hindered, and future discussion will be unlikely.

Brainstorming. This technique often is used during the second phase of discussion sessions, when a class is attempting to secure possible solutions to a problem. However, it's a dynamic interaction device that can be used in any number of Sunday School settings.

Basically, brainstorming is a problem-solving process in which a group attempts to generate as many ideas as possible about a given problem in a short period of time. The most important rule to observe in brainstorming is not to critique any of the comments as they are given.

To get started, state a question or a problem for which you need a variety of good ideas to evaluate. Let's stay with the topic of parent/teen communication. Appoint two persons to write down suggestions concerning how to reach your teenager on a chalkboard or flip chart. By having two people do this, each recorder can quickly write down every other suggestion— which often is needed when ideas start flying.

State the following ground rules to the class before they begin. Group members are to: (1) Give suggestions or ideas as quickly as possible. (2) Say anything that comes to mind, even if it seems silly. (3) Not make any evaluative or judgmental comments during the brainstorming.

You will want to set a short, specified time for this activity. When that time has expired, or when suggestions cease, evaluate each of the suggestions individually and weed out weak or inappropriate ones (such as Mark Twain's suggestion that all teenagers should be sealed in a barrel and fed through the hole). Then discuss the remaining possibilities and try to settle on the best solution.

Buzz Groups. Used to promote dynamic interaction, buzz groups are small groups of four to six students that meet for a brief period of time to discuss a particular topic. A leader is appointed to guide the discussion and another person is asked to record the decisions so that a report can be presented to the entire class. Buzz groups differ from brainstorming groups in that there is not as much emphasis here on coming up with a volume of suggestions.

Buzz groups are particularly helpful when a class is so large that some students feel intimidated to speak out. By subdividing into smaller groups, everyone has an opportunity to participate and excellent involvement is obtained.

Sometimes all groups will be given the same question to discuss; at other times, each group will receive its own individual topic. The choice is up to you, the Sunday School teacher.

In all these dynamic methods, the goal is to secure as much student involvement as possible. In particular, your aim is to promote learner interaction with the lesson content and suggest relevant means of personal application. In this way, you will stimulate interest and learning will be achieved.

The Value of Involvement

Many teachers are aware that dynamic involvement provides great opportunities for effective teaching. Unfortunately, many, if not most teachers, fail to take advantage of opportunities for dynamic involvement. As we mentioned earlier, it's easy for a teacher to see himself as the source of information and the classroom as the place where that information is dispensed. If this is a teacher's perception of teaching, he will be hesitant to plan and use dynamic methods. Perhaps he feels that if dynamic involvement is used, *less* information will wind up being taught; after all, how can students learn anything if they're talking with one another? But both experience and research contradict this conclusion.

Studies have demonstrated a marked improvement in student retention when dynamic methods are used. In fact, one study indicated that dynamic involvement can be twice as effective as the best sensory communication; it can be as much as ten times as effective as a straight lecture (even if you lecture very quickly). Who among us would not like to see our teaching effectiveness increase ten times? The good news is, we *can* do it—by effectively using methods that promote interaction.

The fact remains, however, that the average teacher feels he must "give content" in the class session. If he doesn't cover all the material, he feels guilty. It is of some help to remember, though, that what the *teacher* does in class is relatively insignificant. It is the Holy Spirit's application of biblical truths in the lives of the *learners* that is most important. And that application must continue on into the student's life for lessons *really* to be learned.

Teachers of God's Word have been given the most important task in the world. As stewards responsible to our Master, God will hold us accountable for our faithfulness. We dare not waste time by simply *telling* learners what they need to know. Rather, we must design learning experiences that will have an impact on students' lives—the kinds of experiences that will help them retain content and apply it to life. Then they will know *and* do what God desires. Through this kind of teaching, students can become what God wants them to be. If we are faithful now in our teaching responsibility, someday God will be able to greet each and every one of us with the words, "Well done, good and faithful servant!"

Application Activities

(1) In Matthew, we read that Christ questioned His disciples, saying, "Who do people say that the Son of man is?" (16:13) Why do you think Christ took this approach?

---

(2) What do you think might happen if the teachers in your Christian Education programs concentrated on using interactive methods?

_____

_____

_____

(3) List several reasons why you believe teachers fail to use interactive methods in their classes.

_____

_____

_____

_____

_____

_____

_____

(4) What methods were used most commonly by the Sunday School personnel who taught you? What effect does that have on your approach to teaching?

_____

_____

For suggestions on teaching methods using group dynamics consult: Martha Leypoldt, *Forty Ways to Teach in Groups* (Judson Press), or Kenneth Gangel, *Twenty-four Ways to Improve Your Teaching* (Victor Books).

CHAPTER
SEVEN
MAKING
CONTACT
WITH
STUDENTS

Some time ago I asked a teacher how his Sunday School class was progressing. "I wish I knew," he replied. "But my students never say anything. They just sit there and stare at me. Sometimes I feel as though I'm teaching the Great Stone Face."

The "Great Stone Face" to which my friend referred is a geologic formation found in the mountains of New England. Gazing at this stone resemblance of a man's profile can be a delightful experience. But when the students you're teaching are totally unresponsive, looking at stone faces is anything *but* enjoyable.

Another teacher described similar feelings. One Sunday, he felt he was really communicating with his students; every eye in the room was riveted on him. *Wow,* he thought, *Do I ever have their attention!* But as he moved off to one side of his lectern he noticed that every eye was still focused on the same spot. They were staring, glassy-eyed, at nothing. The Great Stone Face had struck again!

It doesn't have to be that way. We don't need to endure the

agony of thinking—or fearing—that we may be boring our students. Of course, we who teach children usually know immediately when they get bored. When children become bored, they tune out the teacher and start doing something else.

Older youths and adults usually are different. Most of them have learned to be polite when they get bored. So they just sit there quietly and courteously. The teacher must be observant enough to recognize what is happening (or more accurately, *not* happening).

It is terribly important for a teacher constantly to keep in mind what teaching is all about. Teaching is not merely maintaining silence in the classroom. It is not entertaining students. It is not killing time until the bell rings. For a Christian, Sunday School teaching is cooperating with God in helping learners to understand what He wants them to know, and then to become what He wants them to be.

There are many different approaches to planning and teaching a Sunday School lesson. But the three-step approach we will consider in this chapter, and refer to throughout the rest of the book, is one of the simplest and most effective.

Step One involves *making contact* with the learners. Teachers must capture their students' attention as the session begins.

Step Two is *directing* learners to the Word of God so that they can discover what God wants them to know.

Step Three is *guiding* learners to apply those truths to their lives. This enables them to serve God.

Step One: Making Contact

Our ultimate goal (step three) is helping learners to become more like Jesus Christ. But to get to that crucial step, the teacher must start—logically enough—at the beginning. He must work to establish contact with learners. This means knowing them well enough to understand how they think and feel as well as recognizing what interests them.

Many Sunday School teachers know what they, as teachers, are interested in; unfortunately, they often assume—incorrectly—that their students are interested in the same things. As a result, a teacher may begin the class session by addressing his *own* needs or interests, rather than those of his students. In forgetting that his students have a variety of needs, he is losing an important opportunity to make contact with them. Making contact, then, means beginning a Sunday School class session by focusing on things that are of concern to *students*.

I'm sure you've noticed that the first minute or so of a TV show is inevitably fast-paced, exciting, and captivating. The producers know that if they can get you hooked in the first minute, you probably will continue to watch the entire show. The wise teacher should recognize that the same dynamic affects the classroom. Starting a class session with a highly interesting and attractive anecdote or story will grab your learners' attention. Achieving this one goal can pay rich dividends throughout the rest of the session.

Step Two: Directing Learners to the Word
Obviously, the ultimate goal of teaching is not merely to capture your learners' attention and channel their interests. The goals of teaching extend far beyond providing entertainment for students. We need to be committed to the fact that God has revealed Himself and His will for us through the Bible. Thus, because Scripture is the foundation of intelligent faith, we need to help our students learn its contents.

Regrettably, some teachers act as though *teaching* the Bible is the same thing as *talking* about the Bible. In reality, what learners discover for themselves often has far more impact than what we as teachers tell them. This means that to be effective in step two, we need to plan methods and techniques which will direct students to the Word of God. They then can discover for themselves what God has communicated and what He expects of us. Chapter 8 will outline specific ways to help learners study the Bible.

Step Three: Guiding Learners in Application

Even when we *have* captured our learners' attention, and then directed them to the Word of God, a teacher's work still is not finished. We also must guide those learners into practical applications of biblical principles. As we learned in earlier chapters, true biblical knowledge can never be purely theoretical. To know God's Word as He expects us to know it, is to practice God's Word. Only when we do what the Lord expects of us have we actually learned biblical lessons.

Unless we take learners beyond the first two steps to this third step we have not really taught. Biblical instruction must lead to changes in the learners' lives. Their daily behavior must demonstrate the fact that they are new creatures in Jesus Christ. Then, and only then, can we honestly say that they know the truth of God's Word.

Finding a Point of Contact

Recently, while talking with a teenager, I asked him to tell me about his Sunday School class. His response was terse and to the point: "It was the pits!" Rather than accept such a generalization, I asked him to elaborate.

Obliging me, he described his class of the previous Sunday. More than half of his classmates were ignoring the teacher. They were chatting among themselves and doing other things. He went on to explain that the teacher had spent the entire hour talking about a non-Christian religion which was unfamiliar to the class; moreover, the teacher never bothered to define key terms and concepts he was using. As a result, even those students who *were* paying attention were confused.

This teacher had violated two cardinal rules of Sunday School teaching. Both related to his failure to make contact with the learners. His first mistake was that he never got his students' attention. They were interested in other things; and those other things—rather than the lesson—were the focus of their attention. While the teacher knew his topic, and had a genuine concern for his class, he failed to recognize that he and they were traveling on different tracks.

This is not to say that the subject of the lesson or the concepts he taught were irrelevant. They may have been highly relevant. But most of the class members never recognized that relevance. Why? Because the teacher had not made contact. And so he went one way, while most of the class went another.

In failing to make contact, this teacher also made another mistake: he assumed his students' knowledge and experiences were similar to his. He used terms and concepts that were quite familiar to him, but which were unknown to his students. The results were evident: as the class progressed, confusion reigned.

Earlier in this book, I mentioned that the introductory portion of a Sunday School lesson is important to the learning process. The reason for the introduction's importance now should be clear. Basically, it is intended to establish a *point of contact* with learners. When a teacher establishes contact through a proper introduction, he will avoid both of the mistakes cited above. A well-designed introduction will enable a teacher to secure the attention of his learners and help him build on the students' prior knowledge. Then the teacher can lead those students forward to greater learning.

The Role of the Introduction

It's easy to see how the introduction fulfills the first of these purposes. A good, thoroughly prepared introduction will grab the learners' attention. Instead of thinking and talking about a wide variety of unrelated-to-class subjects, students will focus on the same idea. The teacher then can move to his second goal: making contact.

Perhaps the entire function of the introduction can be summed up in a construction analogy. Before building a house, an adequate foundation must be laid. This is the base upon which all subsequent materials will be assembled. If a builder fails to lay the foundation, or if the foundation is weak, the house will be unstable and worthless.

Recently in our town, a contractor was making good progress in constructing a new church building. But one day we noticed that activity had ground to a halt. We soon found out that a city inspector had discovered the poured concrete was defective. Until the weak base was replaced, no more work could be done.

The introduction of a Sunday School lesson is like the foundation of a building. It is the base upon which we build all subsequent instruction. Perhaps we should hire "introduction inspectors" in Christian education. No lesson can be taught until the introduction is approved and found to be adequate. Unless the introduction helps to lead students *into* the lesson, it must be marked "unfit for use."

In discussing the importance of a lesson's introduction, it is crucial to note that we have assumed several things. First, we've assumed that the teacher clearly has thought through the Bible lesson he wants to teach. In other words, he knows both the content and the application he wants to communicate. Then, when the content is known, the teacher can prepare an introduction. We're considering the introduction at this point in the book simply because it comes first during classtime. It should not come first, however, in preparation time.

The second assumption at work here is that the teacher knows those whom he is teaching. Even if the content is well prepared, unless a teacher also knows his students well, he will have great difficulty in communicating effectively. Not only will a teacher have problems at the beginning of the class hour, but those difficulties will continue right on through the entire session. The students may even leave class feeling much the same as the teen who described his class to me. They may very well describe their class as "the pits."

Understanding Learners

Understanding a viewpoint which differs from your own can sometimes be a frustrating experience. Each of us has a unique perspective that influences how we understand others and communicate with them. Often, though, these perspectives become barriers to communication.

When we teach, our task is to overcome such barriers and to guide learners through the teaching/learning process. But to do that, we must understand our students. This involves more than knowing their names and their unique characteristics.

When I was a full-time college professor, I often spent my summers co-directing youth camps. I remember one camp where one of our young charges simply could not be controlled. He was constantly in trouble and had become the subject of more than one early-morning staff meeting. But near the end of the week that he was spending at the camp, this boy and I had some time alone to talk. And talk he did! In those few minutes, I learned an unbelievable amount of information about his problems.

At the staff meeting the next morning, I asked the staff to tell me what they thought of this boy—which they gladly did. After they all had a chance to ventilate, I asked if they had any idea why he acted the way he did. When no one offered any suggestions, I shared what I had learned the previous day. His father had been sentenced to a long prison term just before the boy had left for camp. The church had "kicked out" his entire family because of the scandal. The boy had been told that his father couldn't possibly be a Christian if he were a criminal. And our "problem" camper was questioning whether he could be a believer either.

By the time I finished relating what I had uncovered, there wasn't a dry eye in the room. All of us felt miserable because we had gotten irritated at his behavior without ever taking the time to get to know the boy *behind* the behavior. He was about to leave camp and we'd have no further opportunities to minister to him. I prayed that I'd never forget the lesson I learned that day. Behavior may be more an *expression* of a problem than an *actual* problem itself.

But to understand the root cause of any given problem, we must get to know the person. All of us who teach must get to know individual students. We can't simply teach an amorphous group of students "out there." Yet this usually requires more time and effort than many teachers are willing to give. And getting to know students probably won't happen during classtime on Sunday mornings. It will require an investment of energy and time outside the classroom. Still, as we get to know our students, we *can* transform our teaching.

Are you the type of Sunday School teacher for whom this challenge sounds exciting? Then read on! The following paragraphs outline several suggestions that can help you get to know your students better.

(1) Spend time with learners outside of class. Any teacher who thinks that third-grade boys normally go around wearing shined shoes, shirts and ties, and sport coats has only observed them in Sunday School. Those same boys—on a picnic, playing soccer, canoeing, or having dessert in your home—are totally different creatures. It's in those environments that you'll see the real boy. So unless you spend time together outside of class, you may never see the real person emerge.

(2) Listen to your class. Some teachers are so busy talking that they never take time to listen. It's amazing what you can learn about people when you listen to them. Plan some time alone with your students. Prepare some questions that you want to ask them. Then listen to what they have to say.

One excellent way to learn about young people is to listen to their conversations as you're driving them someplace. For some reason, in the mind of a young person, an adult driver often is viewed as an inanimate part of the "equipment." If you listen to the conversations of a carload of kids, you will learn a great deal about how they think and feel. This information will help you plan effective introductions.

(3) Read what they read. Ask class members what books and magazines they read regularly, then secure copies of them from your local library. For those teachers who work with children or young people, this may mean reading the types of things they read for fun, or selections from school assignments. For adults, you may need to read articles that relate to their hobbies or interests, as well as material they read for work. As a result of your efforts, you'll be better equipped to understand where your students' interests lie. This, in turn, will enable you to select illustrations that will be meaningful to the individuals you teach.

(4) Sit in on other classes. If you teach children, visit a public elementary or secondary school class. Or visit the childrens' class at another church. If you teach adults, sit in on a home Bible study or attend a seminar with class members. But don't attend merely to study the material they're using. Attend to study *the students*. Observe what methods the teacher uses, and watch to see how the learners respond. You may get ideas on how you can improve your own communication style or on how your class members respond to various teaching styles and methods.

(5) Become a people-watcher. Observe members of the age-group you teach to understand how they communicate their feelings. Try observing their conversations from a distance to see if you can figure out what they are saying through their body language. Learn to recognize how they communicate feelings and emotions, and thereby become increasingly sensitive

to messages they send to each other and to you.

Methods of Making Contact

Some teachers realize how important it is to make contact with learners at the beginning of the class session. But they don't always know how to do it. All good Sunday School curriculum publishers include suggestions for planning effective introductions. You should consider these and tailor them for effective use with your class. For your immediate convenience, the following suggestions describe several highly effective approaches to planning introductions for good initial contact in class:

(1) Address Felt Needs. We previously considered the advantages of being able to speak to a felt need. A felt need is one the learner knows he has, and for which he is seeking a solution. We're all aware that people have needs. But often, they have not yet recognized some of their greatest ones. A teacher, therefore, must help students recognize real needs.

For example, everyone needs to be spiritually reborn; Christ offers salvation through His death and resurrection. But many people do not realize that they need salvation. A Sunday School teacher can play a vital role in clarifying that need and identifying its remedy.

Because we all are complex individuals, sometimes it is very difficult for a teacher to recognize specific student needs. But the better we know learners, the better we will understand their real needs. Then we can help our students recognize those needs by addressing them in class.

(2) Challenge Learners. All of us can do more and learn more than we give ourselves credit for. Wise teachers look for ways to challenge students through their introductions. Sometimes this can take the form of a goal to reach or a problem to solve. Many times we want to do too much for learners, rather than challenging them and then letting them work on their own.

After Christ gave His disciples their basic instruction, He sent them out, knowing how much they were going to have to stretch to meet the challenge. Consider some of the trials they were to face:

I send you as sheep in the midst of wolves (Matt. 10:16).

They will deliver you up (v. 17).

And you will be hated by all on My account (v. 22).

But whenever they persecute you in this city, flee to the next (v. 23).

But Christ knew that such challenges were necessary—and His disciples rose to the occasion. They returned ready to learn more and to be sent to the Gentiles. We do our learners a grave disservice if we fail to challenge them to reach for their potential.

(3) Appeal to Curiosity. Everyone is curious. We can take advantage of this attribute in planning good introductions. Good teachers often begin with a question to stimulate learner curiosity. Another effective technique is to cite examples or illustrations that will encourage the learner to look further for an answer or resolution to a situation. "Why does this work?" "Why was a person able to respond that way?" "Why do we act like this or respond like that?" Look for ways to draw learners into the teaching/learning process by sharing ideas that will pique their curiosity.

(4) Set up Tension or Present a Paradox. The Bible contains many concepts that seem to contradict one another, or that contradict popular ideas. Introducing these tensions to your Sunday School students may help to draw them into the learning process. "He who would save his life must lose it," or "The

first shall be last," are illustrations of seemingly contradictory ideas. As we look, it will become increasingly easy to find biblical concepts that contradict popular (secular or church) wisdom. These conflicts help create stimulating and effective introductions for classes. And they will help you make contact with learners.

In conclusion, the introduction to a lesson can be likened to a launching pad. If you don't get off the pad, the lesson rarely will go anywhere. In the early years of our space program, Cape Canaveral was the scene of many failures. Some even dubbed it "Malfunction Junction." But our scientists learned from those mistakes and were able to correct them.

In the past, your introductions may have left much to be desired. But let's move beyond those experiences and learn how to plan effective introductions to get those lessons up and going.

Application Activities

(1) Some media analysts have estimated that more effort is devoted to the first minute of a TV show than to any other portion. What percentage of preparation time do you think should be devoted to planning the introduction of a lesson? Why?

_____

_____

_____

(2) Put yourself in the place of your students. What kinds of techniques do you think would be most effective in capturing your attention at the beginning of a class session?

_____

(3) Why do teachers who spend a substantial amount of time in preparation often neglect to plan an introduction?

_____

_____

_____

(4) Make a list of things you could do with individual learners to get to know them better.

_____

_____

_____

_____

_____

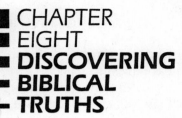

CHAPTER EIGHT
DISCOVERING BIBLICAL TRUTHS

When I was a high school student I studied Latin. It was, to say the least, a trying experience. And so my classmates and I felt terribly clever when we composed what we thought was an original poem:

> The Latin language is dead,
>   As dead as dead can be.
> First it killed the Romans,
>   And now it's killing me.

You can imagine the great disillusionment I experienced when my father told me he had recited the same poem "hundreds of years" earlier when *he* studied Latin. Back then, his feelings about Latin had been similar to mine. We both questioned the practicality of studying such an ancient language and wound up deciding it was useless—totally irrelevant for people living in the twentieth century.

Many times, however, I have been extremely grateful for that language study. No, I don't speak Latin to my friends. But it has proven valuable as I study other languages, and has helped me to improve my grasp of English. If only I had recognized those values as a freshman in high school! I would have gained far more from my study of Latin had my attitude been better.

Unfortunately, many people relegate the Bible to the same category in which I placed the Latin language. They perceive it as dead and useless. Irrelevant and out of date. "After all," they reason, "how could something written thousands of years ago have any significance today?" Some feel that with our vast advances in scientific knowlege, we have moved beyond such "primitive" things.

Even if the Bible *were* only a history book written by humans, it still would be valuable. People who lived during biblical times had insight and understanding that we need today. Their lives were valuable examples and we can profit from their experience.

But the Bible is far more than just a record of human experience. It is eternal and absolute truth, revealed by God for our instruction and guidance. It is both accurate and authoritative. The Bible is the Lord's message to us, and as such, is far more relevant and up-to-date than tonight's newscast or tomorrow's newspaper. God has chosen to reveal both Himself and His expectations for us through His Word, the Bible. And so there is no more important task that Sunday School teachers could undertake than helping others understand what God has said.

Regrettably, many teachers approach the Bible as I approached language instruction. I've termed such an approach the "castor oil school" of study, because as the saying goes, "It may taste terrible, but it's good for you." However, many learners drop out of classes where the "castor oil approach" is followed. Those who *do* endure, who put up with ineffective instruction, still wind up with little zest or enthusiasm for learning.

One Bible scholar has suggested that it is a sin to bore people with God's Word. But we will do exactly that if we merely teach *facts* of ancient history. The facts *are* vitally important, but we must recognize that we are teaching far more than history. We are sharing eternal truths revealed by the Spirit of God—truth that can guide us today.

Jesus' explanation of this principle is recorded in John's Gospel:

If you abide in My Word, then you are truly disciples of Mine; and you shall know the truth, and the truth shall set you free (8:31-32).

Obviously, Christ was emphasizing the importance of knowing the Word. But it is significant that He emphasized *abiding* in the Word. This implies that we need to do more than merely memorize facts. Abiding in the Word means actively seeking to build our lives on the teachings found in the Bible. It means recognizing Scripture as the source of the truth that energizes life. When we do these things, then we are free to live the life that God intended. Our knowledge of the Word, which leads to a deeper knowledge of God, will produce vital growing experiences in our lives.

But this kind of teaching and learning doesn't happen by accident. It comes as a direct result of the approach we take to studying the Bible for ourselves and for teaching it to others. As we teach the *facts* of the Word, we constantly must seek to teach the *principles* those facts reveal.

In order to achieve such effective levels of understanding, we need to recognize two crucial elements in our teaching of the Bible. We must remember the importance of an accurate knowledge of facts, and also recognize the importance of knowing and teaching the principles of the Word of God that are revealed through the facts.

The Importance of Bible Facts

In order to teach the Bible to others, teachers first must understand the Bible for themselves. And to insure an accurate understanding of the facts of the Word, certain principles must be followed. These principles are known as *hermeneutics*. While this term may sound esoteric or foreign to you, almost everyone understands the basic principles of hermeneutics.

For those of us who recognize the Bible as God's Word, three principles summarize the heart of hermeneutics. We believe in literal, grammatical, and historical interpretation. Let's look at each of these points briefly.

(1) Literal interpretation means that we take the Bible at face value. We do not try to invest Scripture with some hidden meaning. When we pick up any other piece of written material, we normally interpret it literally; that is, if it describes some event, we assume the event actually took place, unless evidence indicates it did not.

Of course, I am not ignoring the fact that people often employ figures of speech. When someone says, "I'm so hungry I could eat a horse," we know that person is speaking figuratively to describe terrific hunger. Likewise, the Bible contains a great deal of symbolic language. "The Lord is my shepherd" (Ps. 23:1) means that God relates to me in the way a shepherd relates to his sheep. When Jesus said, "The kingdom of heaven is like a mustard seed" (Matt. 13:31), He was using a simile. He employed a familiar object to describe a less familiar concept.

Literal interpretation recognizes the fact that the writer had an idea to communicate, and that he chose normal methods of written communication to express that idea. When we interpret the Bible literally, poetry should be read as poetry, historical events as history, doctrinal teaching as instruction, and so forth.

(2) Grammatical interpretation means that we must observe the grammatical laws of communication. In speech today, we must use proper tenses, singular or plural forms, agreement of pronouns, etc. to assure accurate communication. The Bible, as written communication, follows these same laws of grammar; we must recognize those laws in interpreting the Bible just as we do any other literature.

Since the Bible was written primarily in Hebrew or Greek, it is to our advantage if we can read those langauges. But the teacher who doesn't read the original languages still can understand the Bible. There are many fine resources (some of which are listed below) written by language scholars who know and understand the grammatical laws of those languages.

(3) Historical interpretation means that we must recognize that biblical events involved real people, living in a historical context. If we remove them from that context, we lose or distort the meaning of Scripture. We always need to ask to whom a particular passage was addressed and what it meant to them. By understanding how they perceived the teaching and how the speaker intended it to be understood, we can better understand the passage ourselves.

Of course, as we seek to use literal, grammatical, and historical interpretation, a logical question is, How can we know exactly what message a particular passage is teaching? The first place to look for such help is the teacher's manual of the curriculum materials you're using. One major purpose for the manual is to help teachers answer that very question. Curriculum materials that do not give help in that basic area are inferior and ought to be rejected.

A second place to look for help is in your own reference books or those that can be borrowed from a library. Though some of these are fairly expensive, several reference books purchased over a period of time will be well worth the investment for a serious teacher. The following are suggested:

(1) A contemporary Bible translation is helpful when the version you most often use seems confusing.

(2) A Bible concordance contains references for all the verses in the Bible. Each verse will be listed several times according to the main words found in that verse.

(3) A topical Bible is similar to a concordance, but verses are listed according to the *concepts* taught in those verses. Sometimes this type of book is called a subject index.

(4) A Bible dictionary explains words, people, places, and events in the Bible. Frequently, it serves as a one-volume Bible encyclopedia.

(5) A one- or two-volume commentary can be very helpful. The main purpose of a commentary is to explain the meaning of various Bible passages. Therefore, it is important to choose one that doesn't ignore or gloss over difficult passages.

Few of us would be able to purchase all of these books at any one time. But by planning ahead, in a surprisingly short period of time a teacher can accumulate a valuable set of reference books.

If you were to hire a plumber, you would expect him to own the tools necessary to do a good job. Suppose he came to you and asked to borrow your tools—a pipe wrench, a propane torch, solder, a wire brush, and gloves. Before long, you would seriously question his competence. A workman without tools probably isn't a very skilled craftsman.

So it is in teaching. If we want to do an excellent job, we should acquire the tools needed to perform our task. When we encounter a particularly difficult passage during our preparation time, those tools will prove priceless.

If we're to help other people understand the Word of God, we ourselves need to know what it means. Then, and only then, are we in a position to share those concepts with others. And when our students have learned the *facts* of the Bible, they will be ready to go on to a deeper understanding of the *principles* of the Bible—and of how those principles apply to their lives.

Teaching Bible Principles

Unfortunately, when Christian educators teach Bible content to their students, some commit a grave error. They assume that when they have taught Bible *facts*, they have done their job. But in such cases, their lessons usually wind up as courses in ancient history; their learners erroneously conclude that the Bible has little application for today. Even if students *do* accept Scripture as the Word of God, and realize it is important to know, they still may fail to understand that biblical truths should guide our lives in the here and now.

The Word of God becomes even more significant to us when we realize that God has chosen to reveal selected truths to us. That is, He has not chosen to record *everything* that ever happened. As John observed:

And there are also many other things which Jesus did, which if they were written in detail, I suppose that even the world itself would not contain the books which were written (John 21:25).

Since only a portion of what Christ (and other biblical characters) did and said was recorded, there must be a reason for our having the material we do. Apparently, God desired us to know certain teachings and events, so He preserved that specific information for us in the Bible. This information is needed to guide us in our life and service for Him.

Therefore, if we want to teach effectively as we communicate Bible facts, we also must teach how and why those facts are important today. We need to teach the principles which those facts represent. Bible facts describe historical events. Bible principles are the eternal truths understood through those facts. These principles reveal the nature and will of God.

But rather than theorizing about the difference between fact and principle, let's look at a specific illustration of how to use both of these elements in our Sunday School teaching:

> Then all the elders of Israel gathered together and came to Samuel at Ramah; and they said to him, "Behold, you have grown old, and your sons do not walk in your ways. Now appoint a king for us to judge us like all the nations." But the thing was displeasing in the sight of Samuel when they said, "Give us a king to judge us." And Samuel prayed to the Lord. And the Lord said to Samuel, "Listen to the voice of the people in regard to all that they say to you, for they have not rejected you, but they have rejected Me from being king over them. Like all the deeds which they have done since the day that I brought them up from Egypt even to this day—in that they have forsaken Me and served other gods— so they are doing to you also. Now then listen to their voice; however, you shall solemnly warn them and tell them of the procedure of the king who will reign over them" (1 Sam. 8:4-9).

After stating this, God revealed to Samuel all the negative things that a king would do to Israel. He warned the people that a king would oppress them and that they would regret their demand:

> Then you will cry out in that day because of your king whom you have chosen for yourselves, but the Lord will not answer you in that day (1 Sam. 8:18).

Unfortunately, the Israelites did not heed God's warning. Instead, they persisted in their demands, and so God gave them a king. This king did everything God had warned the Israelites he would do, and the people cried out for deliverance. But God did not deliver them.

We know that everything in the Bible is true, and this includes the narrative found in 1 Samuel 8. This passage is a historically accurate account, and it is important to teach such facts. But a teacher could teach the facts of 1 Samuel 8 without ever *truly teaching* the passage. To teach the passage fully, a teacher also must teach the principles contained in it.

Several of the principles revealed through this passage are: (1) If we insist on going our own way, God may let us have what we want—to our own detriment. (2) If we refuse to obey God, and get into trouble because of our disobedience, God will not erase that action or reverse the consequences. (3) God's plan for His children is better than any other we could design for ourselves. (4) If we imitate the world which rejects God, we will find ourselves departing from the way He wants us to go.

It is vitally important to teach Bible facts; but we have stopped short of effectively teaching Scripture if we do not teach its principles as well. This is not to say that we have to teach *all* of the principles in any given passage. Ordinarily, there are many more principles in a passage than we can include in a given class. But as we discover new principles each time we study a particular passage of Scripture, we can develop new lesson themes.

Teachers need to be selective in teaching appropriate principles. As you come to know class members better and understand their needs more fully, the Holy Spirit will help you select those principles which will be most beneficial to them. If you are teaching 1 Samuel 8 to junior high students, for example, you should concentrate on the principles they need most. You might focus on the danger of trying to model one's life and expectations after those who do not know God. The Israelites wanted a king because all the other nations had one. If you are teaching Young Adults, you might want to concentrate on the principle of living with the consequence of our choices. After ignoring God's will, when the Israelites called out to God for deliverance, He did not answer.

A teacher who fails to teach the facts of the Word is doing a disservice to his students. He is omitting vital content of eternal value. God has revealed biblical facts, and they are profitable to know. But the teacher who teaches only the facts still is missing the mark. He is teaching the Bible as if it were nothing more than accurate history, and missing the opportunity to show its relevance for life today.

Application Activities

(1) "But prove yourselves doers of the Word, and not merely hearers who delude themselves" (James 1:22). Why did James distinguish between hearing and doing the Word?

_____

_____

_____

(2) When we talk today about "knowing" something, do you think we usually mean "hearing" or "doing" in the sense that Jesus used those terms?_____

_____

_____

_____

(3) Make a list of the resource books already in your possession. Then list those you would like to purchase and stop by a local Christian bookstore to get suggestions of titles and prices for those books. Plan a time schedule for purchasing those books.

_____

_____

_____

_____

_____

_____

_____

_____

(4) Can you suggest principles in addition to those listed above that might be taught from 1 Samuel 8:4-18?

_____

_____

_____

_____

_____

_____

_____

(5) What do you think would happen if a teacher tried to teach the principles of the Word without first teaching the facts?

CHAPTER NINE
RESPONDING TO BIBLICAL TRUTHS

I recently visited with a pastor who told me a terrific real-life anecdote. This story was so good, in fact, he submitted it to *Reader's Digest* and got it published.

One Sunday, a pastor was conducting the children's sermon. This is a time in the worship service when children are invited to the front of the sanctuary to hear a special message. On this particular Sunday, the pastor had planned to conduct a short question-and-answer session with the children. He started by asking them if they knew what was small, had a bushy tail, ran around the lawn, and gathered nuts. Immediately, a boy in the back of the group spoke up. "I know the answer's Jesus," he said, "but it sure sounds like a squirrel to me!"

I found this anecdote amusing because I could clearly visualize the young boy. He has come to think that Christian educators ask only simplistic questions—questions that usually can be answered with the words "God," "Jesus," or "the Bible." They're the kind of responses my eldest son Mark calls "Sunday School answers."

Mark and I have a running disagreement about this particular expression. I dislike it, because superficial answers are not unique to Sunday School. But based on his own observations, Mark maintains that most of the question-and-answer exchanges that occur in Sunday School are extremely shallow. And so, to Mark, all answers that reflect a lack of serious thought are "Sunday School answers"—especially if someone says "Jesus," when the correct answer should be "a squirrel."

Unfortunately, we Sunday School teachers sometimes contribute to encouraging mindless responses from our students. It's important for learners to memorize passages of Scripture. I won't dispute that. But how do we make them do it? Are we satisfied if they rattle off a series of syllables that make up the verse, though they remain totally unaware of the meaning of that passage? Or do we take the time to help students understand both the words *and* their meaning?

I think the answer is obvious. We need to help students grasp the concepts which those biblical words convey. Verbalism (putting together words with no understanding of their meaning) works against true understanding and communication. If we permit (or even encourage) it, we may be guilty of promoting mindless participation. And the net result of our negligence may well be to weaken the impact of the Bible. We actually could be encouraging "Sunday School answers."

Educators look at learning in many different ways, but they generally agree that students move through a *sequence* in learning. For the sake of clarity, perhaps it would be helpful to view learning in terms of climbing a five-limbed tree. A person has begun to climb the tree when he reaches the first limb. But in the deepest sense of the word, he really has not *climbed* the tree until he has achieved the uppermost limb. That's when knowledge is acted out in life. We ought to look, therefore, at each of these limbs (levels) of learning.

(1) The first level consists of **memorizing facts.** When stu-

dents have the ability to remember facts, they're off to a good start. And in this tree, you can't get to the next limb if you try to skip the first. The main problem which develops at the memory level occurs when a Sunday School teacher is satisfied to have his students perpetually perched on this first limb.

(2) Level two is **understanding principles.** At this level, facts are perceived as more than just facts; they're seen as the building blocks of ideas. And understanding those ideas, or principles, is a key to meaningful learning. The ability to remember facts and to put them together coherently requires better developed cognitive skills than exist at level one. But there still are more limbs to come!

(3) The third level involves **realizing implications for life.** This limb requires the learner to exercise significantly more insight than the two previous ones. It extends beyond remembering facts and understanding the principles those facts represent. At this level, the learner realizes that the facts God has communicated are intended to reveal principles that can guide our lives today. Such insight is necessary before a person truly can progress from "hearing the Word" to "doing the Word" (James 1:25).

(4) Level four, **choosing to obey,** now is within the student's reach. This limb represents an act of the will. It requires more than remembering—or even understanding a particular fact. This is the stage at which learners make a choice either to obey God or to reject His demands. This is the limb where each student is able to respond to the convincing work of the Holy Spirit.

And He [the Holy Spirit], when He comes, will convict the world concerning sin, and righteousness, and judgment (John 16:9).

But convicting (or convincing) does not mean that a learner

automatically responds to what God expects. Deciding to respond is an individual choice—an act of the will. We teachers must permit learners the freedom to make that choice. The learner himself must take hold of that limb.

(5) The fifth and final level is **changing behavior.** When the learner achieves this limb, he finally has climbed the learning tree. While he may have been in the tree all along, the learner has not *really* learned until the truths communicated by the facts actually have been incorporated into his life. At this level the learner remembers the facts, understands the principles that those facts communicate, realizes their implications for his life, chooses to obey them, and actually does what God wants him to do. In the fullest sense of the word, he has learned the lesson!

Applying Biblical Principles

One of the best-known and most-loved college football coaches was the University of Alabama's Paul "Bear" Bryant. Under Coach Bryant's leadership, the Crimson Tide was known and feared for its running game. In fact, Bryant's emphasis on running the football gave rise to one of his more quoted sayings: "When you pass the football, three things can happen, and two of them are bad." His point was, when a player attempts a pass, the ball might be caught—or, it could fall incomplete or be intercepted.

A similar principle relates to applying lessons. When you fail to help your students understand how biblical principles apply to life, three things can happen, and two of them are bad. While learners sometimes make valid applications on their own, they also may misapply the principles or not apply them at all. Thus, two out of the three possibilities are bad.

A few moments ago, we considered the need to help learners discover God's truth. This responsibility involves the first two levels of learning—remembering facts and understanding principles. While these two accomplishments are crucial, they are not the end of learning. True learning requires further achievement. It is important that learners apply the biblical principles to life.

The three upper limbs on the tree of learning relate to learner response. Learners need to realize the implications for life (level 3), choose to obey (level 4), and actually change their behavior (level 5). While all of these activities are learner-centered, the teacher plays a crucial role in each one. Let's start by considering how the teacher assists at level 3.

Level 3: Realizing Implications for Life

The teacher obviously plays an important part at this level. Generally, it is the teacher who suggests how a particular biblical truth relates to contemporary life. This is not too difficult to do if the teacher clearly has taught both the facts *and* the principles which those Bible facts communicate. Bible principles are eternal truths that apply to all generations.

Earlier, we considered the facts of 1 Samuel 8, which recounted Israel's rejection of God's rule through the judges. We also understood that those facts communicated certain principles about God and His dealings with us. Learners are able to realize the implications of those principles when they're shown how to apply them to life. One exciting aspect of Sunday School teaching, then, is recognizing the various ways that a given principle can be applied to different age-groups. For instance, a principle we earlier considered from the 1 Samuel passage—that of the consequences of rejecting God's plan—could apply to children, youth, and adults.

If you are teaching children, you might emphasize the importance of obeying parents and the consequences of disobedience. If you are teaching youth, you might emphasize decisions regarding the choice of a career or a life partner. Adults could understand the principle as it applies to fidelity to one's spouse or the use of spiritual gifts in service. All of these applications could grow out of the same biblical principle.

It is important for a teacher to realize that the *facts* of a given passage of Scripture have one particular meaning. An understanding of facts will not differ from one person to another. But once we understand the meaning of the facts in a particular Bible passage, we can recognize that a variety of *principles* devolve from them. Obviously, the principles will not contradict each other, but will emphasize different aspects of that passage. Moreover, there can be countless applications of those principles. It is up to you, the Sunday School teacher, to emphasize applications that are most relevant to a particular class.

To sum up, there is one interpretation of facts, numerous principles, and countless applications relative to any given Bible passage. These points explain why the Bible applies to all people at any time in history.

The problem confronting a teacher is how to select the best illustrations to help his particular group of learners apply the passage's truths. The first place to begin searching for ways to apply your lesson is in the teacher's manual of the curriculum materials you're using. Since it has been written for a specific age-group, it will suggest applications for that age-group. Of necessity, these will be general suggestions, since the writers do not know your students personally. So feel free to adapt and modify their suggestions. Sunday School teachers always should seek those illustrations which relate best to their students.

Another good source of illustrations is the general experiences that are common to the age-group you're teaching. If you are instructing young people, for example, you should know what is going on in their school. Acquaint yourself with the types of problems and difficulties they face. Learn about their teachers, their classes, and their athletic teams. Take time to find out what activities and ideas are popular with these students and their peers. Then choose illustrations that relate well to their lives and experiences. Five of the seven sixth-grade boys that I presently teach are avid soccer players. You can imagine what kind of illustrations I often use.

You also will discover good illustration ideas from the specific problems and personal experiences of learners in your class. But in order to use this source, you must get to know class members personally. They must feel free to share with you. And you must have their confidence.

One word of caution in using illustrations that you derive from your class members' lives. You must never embarrass learners or reveal confidences. If you want to use a personal illustration from someone in your class, always ask his or her permission first. At times, it might be best to take a specific illustration, and then generalize it. In other words, "change the names and places to protect the innocent."

The better we come to know the general characteristics of the age- or interest-group we teach, the more relevant our teaching will be. Knowing learners personally will increase our effectiveness even more.

Level 4: Choosing to Obey

As much as we might wish it were possible, Sunday School teachers cannot do the learning for their students. Individual students must decide for themselves how much they want to learn. It is up to them to choose how far and how fast they wish to progress. Some learners will earnestly desire to move rapidly through all five steps of the learning process. They'll be eager to dwell in the uppermost limbs of the tree.

Few things are as satisfying to a teacher as the student who delights in learning. And believe it or not, such persons *do* exist. Some, perhaps from a very early age, have been imbued with a love for learning and a thirst for knowledge. Such learners need only scant encouragement from their teacher. This kind of student often will stretch his teacher beyond belief.

Unfortunately, another variety of student also exists. While highly motivated learners strive for limb five, reluctant learners seem intent on avoiding the shadow of the tree! Some of these students may have had negative experiences and now think that learning is unpleasant or distasteful. Consequently, they spend their time resisting all attempts at education. While others are drinking deeply at the fountain of knowledge, these persons don't even care to gargle.

We must relate carefully to such individuals. We must make ourselves particularly available to them for encouragement and inspiration, because these students *can* learn too. But as we offer support and encouragement, we must allow the student to choose to learn for himself. It is at learning levels four and five—deciding to change and then actually changing behavior—where this freedom of decision is most crucial. No person can make decisions for another individual. Each learner must choose whether or not he wants to change his own behavior.

This is not to say, though, that a student should be left standing alone in making these decisions. We have considered before how the Holy Spirit plays a vital role in convincing a person of the truth of God's Word. This ministry of the Spirit is vital in a learner's decision to obey God.

Yet the teacher can play a vital role here also. Even though he cannot make a decision for the learner, a teacher still contributes to the process. The *example* which a godly teacher presents can itself encourage a learner to decide to obey God. Paul wrote that he was sure Timothy would continue in what he had learned because of his teacher's influence:

You, however, continue in the things you have learned and become convinced of, knowing from whom you have learned them (2 Tim. 3:14).

The character of a teacher, expressed through a variety of relationships, is vital in drawing students to the place where they choose to obey God. Upon reflection, many Christians have realized that they committed themselves to Christ because they were impressed by the genuine concern of a Sunday School teacher. God used the personal impact of a teacher to lead those persons to respond to the call of the Spirit of God. Paul recognized that the special quality of a teacher/student relationship often mirrors the relationship shared by parents and children:

> I do not write these things to shame you, but to admonish you as my beloved children. For if you were to have countless tutors in Christ, yet you would not have many fathers; for in Christ Jesus I became your father through the Gospel. I exhort you therefore, be imitators of me (1 Cor. 4:14-16).

Highly effective teaching, in other words, closely approximates parenting. The tutor referred to in 1 Corinthians was a person (often a trusted slave) who would escort a student to school. He was not a teacher in the truest sense of the word, but a servant who performed a routine function. The tutor made sure that a student was physically present at instruction sessions. He was sort of a first-century truant officer.

This illustration offers a challenge to us as teachers. We can and should be more than just functional "slaves." Rather than performing the routine act of "manipulating a learner" into contact with information, teachers ought to have a personal desire to nurture learners. It is through this personal relationship and genuine concern that a teacher can exert influence over his students. Teachers can help them to achieve level four—deciding to change. Then students are well prepared to move on to level five—actually changing behavior as God desires. Only as students move on to level five can we say that they really have *learned* the Bible truth.

Level 5: Changing Behavior

The fact that I'm devoting a short space to this final application level does not imply that it's unimportant. It is, perhaps, the *most* crucial part of the entire teaching/learning process. For even though teaching may begin in the class, true application takes place outside the classroom. The final level of learning leads a student to practice godly obedience for the rest of his life. What happens in the formal learning context will lay the foundation for this lifelong application. And as we've noted throughout this book, two specific relationships will make the application most effective.

The first is the relationship that a teacher has developed with a student. If a teacher truly has built a parenting relationship, then a learner will welcome his encouragement and suggestions. As specific problems of application arise, the learner will look to his teacher for guidance. The teacher may then play a continuing role in such cases, acting more as a counselor than a teacher.

The second relationship (and the more important of the two) is the student's ongoing relationship with God. Paul wrote:

So then, my beloved, just as you have always obeyed, not as in my presence only, but now much more in my absence, work out your salvation with fear and trembling; for it is God who is at work within you, both to will and to work for His good pleasure (Phil. 2:12-13).

Teachers must recognize that the only behavioral change of lasting value occurs when a person chooses to allow God to control his life. The Spirit of God will not only motivate a person's *desire* to change, He will provide the *power* to actually obey God. A learner cannot talk himself into obedience. But he can allow God to work in and through his life, making this final level of learning a continuing achievement. Rather than simply accumulating a great quantity of information from his Sunday School education, a learner will be growing and maturing to God's glory.

Application Activities

(1) Why are teachers often willing to accept empty, meaningless answers from their students?

_____

_____

_____

(2) What kind of an attitude toward the Bible might a person develop if he receives only "factual" biblical instruction? How can this be avoided?

_____

_____

_____

(3) Why do some teachers fail to use illustrations that grow out of the life experiences of the students they teach?

_____

_____

_____

(4) How do you react to the following statement: "The Bible is totally relevant, but our teaching may be irrelevant"?

_____

_____ _____

_____

(5) How would you feel if one of your students rejected your instruction and chose not to obey God? What could you do about it?

_____

_____

_____

(6) How much time do you think elapses before a teacher can recognize the results of his instruction?

_____

_____

_____

_____

CHAPTER TEN
PUTTING YOUR LESSON TOGETHER

The story is told of a man who was practicing target-shooting in his backyard. When a friend came over to visit, he noticed that every shot had landed exactly in the middle of the target's bull's eye. The visitor marveled at how anyone could be so consistent in his shooting. Intrigued, he asked the marksman how he had managed to shoot so many bull's eyes. "It's easy," the man replied. "All I do is shoot first. *Then* I draw the target."

Unfortunately, some teachers appear to attempt something similar in their classrooms. They never get around to selecting appropriate lesson goals ahead of time, so they just sort of make things up as they go along. At the end of class, they might even tell you that everything worked out exactly the way they wanted it to! But whether you're target-shooting or teaching, setting goals after the fact doesn't work. Excellent Sunday School teachers *plan* to achieve certain objectives with their learners—and then they work toward accomplishing those predetermined goals.

In the preceding chapters we have considered many aspects

of the teaching/learning process. In this chapter, we will examine steps which teachers can follow in preparing a Sunday School lesson, and consider how they can direct their teaching toward specific goals.

Let's start by looking at the process of lesson preparation.

Step One

I'm assuming that if you're reading this book, you're a teacher (or potential teacher) who will be sharing God's Word. Therefore, to teach the Bible effectively, you need to begin by studying the facts of the Word. Even though you will be using prepared curriculum materials in class, start by studying the biblical facts on which your lesson will be based.

Go to the Bible and familiarize yourself with the appropriate passage. One of the best ways to do this is to read the passage repeatedly. Many teachers prefer to begin their lesson preparation early in the week so they can review the passage many times during the ensuing days. As you read, write down ideas as they come to you. Later, these concepts or thoughts may be included in your actual lesson.

One of the great Bible scholars from the first half of the twentieth century, G. Campbell Morgan, once stated that until a person has read a passage fifty times, he has not even *begun* to study it. That view probably is a bit extreme for many of us. But then few of us will ever be called the "Prince of Bible Expositors," as Morgan was. The purpose of repeated reading is simply to familiarize yourself with the facts; as we saw in the last chapter, you cannot understand scriptural principles until you know the facts of the Bible. The more often you read a passage, the more questions you'll find coming to mind. To answer those questions, refer to your teacher's manual or use the reference books you have begun acquiring. Understanding crucial biblical facts will increase your confidence as you teach. And increased confidence will increase your effectiveness.

Step Two

The second step in preparing your lesson is to recognize the biblical principles which the passage contains. Once you have a basic grasp of the facts, principles will begin to emerge. These are the concepts, revealed through the facts, that describe how God relates to His creation and how we should respond to Him. Remember that even though a passage may not be written directly to the church, its principles still may apply to us.

Consider the siege of Jericho. God's command for Joshua's army to march around the walls of the city, to shout, and to blow trumpets was not written directly to us. But the facts of this story reveal many principles. One of these, for example, might be God's expectation of obedience. Even if an action does not seem wise from a human point of view, God still expects His orders to be obeyed.

A teacher ordinarily will discover many principles in a Scripture portion—more than could reasonably be covered in one session. But again, your teacher's manual will prove an invaluable source for winnowing out suggested principles. Just be sure that the principles you eventually teach are legitimately derived from the verses you're considering. We must not "read into" a passage things which are not taught in that specific portion of Scripture.

Step Three

The third step in effective preparation is to select the principles that apply most directly to the students you're teaching. This is where a knowledge of both the Word of God and your learners is so important. While there may be a number of principles you could teach, you ought to select those that your class needs most.

The principles you plan to emphasize also will determine your lesson's aims. An aim is the goal of your teaching—it's what you want to see happen in your students' lives. Some teachers make the mistake of expecting only a learner's *knowledge* to change. As a result, they plan their lessons so that learners wind up with a greater accumulation of *facts*. But think back to the learning tree. As we saw there, remembering facts is important—but it represents only the bottom limb of education. The final goal of teaching should be a change in *behavior*. Therefore, it is vitally important to determine lesson aims or goals that relate to the problems, needs, or daily activities of the learners.

While this may seem to be a small matter, stating an aim properly often will have a marked influence on the effectiveness of your teaching. A good aim will help you to target your instruction. A little later in this chapter, we'll consider some ways to ensure that your aim is effective.

Planning Your Approach

Teaching the Bible can be a very satisfying and rewarding experience. This is particularly true when a teacher spends an adequate amount of time studying and preparing his material. Likewise, it's exciting to get to know learners and then to see them grow and mature.

But not every teaching experience is rewarding, and not all teachers are satisfied or excited. Why not? Sometimes, it's because a teacher has not spent enough time studying the Word. Any teacher who is unprepared will find the classroom experience quite frustrating; that teacher will approach his class feeling insecure and hesitant. Questions from the students will be something to avoid, rather than to encourage.

While a teacher who spends inadequate time studying the Bible can expect to encounter problems in class, teachers who *do* spend time studying may *still* find that their teaching has little effect. Their learners will continue to be passive nonparticipants. Why?

Often, the problem is a very simple one to solve. Let's consider an analogy. Suppose that you're planning to entertain guests for dinner. You want this dinner to be something special, so you go to the best supermarket in town. You carefully analyze the contents of product after product, choosing only those which measure up to your high standards. Only the freshest produce will do, and the meat you select is the best cut available. You finally arrive at home with an assortment of the finest ingredients imaginable. You feel satisfied that the evening will be a smashing success.

Shortly before the guests arrive, you get out the largest kettle in your kitchen, set it on the stove, and dump all your purchases into it. As it boils away you anticipate the delight of your guests, knowing that you're about to serve them a dinner of high-quality ingredients. At the appointed time, you remove the kettle from the stove, place it on the table, and prepare to watch your guests "dig in."

But something is wrong. Your dinner companions don't seem excited. In fact, they appear to have no appetites at all. So you pass the kettle around again. But no one takes a second helping. Before long, your guests graciously excuse themselves and depart. They have been courteous—but cool—and your sense of excitement has waned considerably. How could they reject such fine food? Why did they seem so disinterested when you served them the best ingredients available?

The problem was not your guests' dislike of the ingredients. The problem was in how you *presented* the meal. Even the most nutritious food must be prepared carefully and presented appropriately to be appreciated. Slopping it all in a kettle just won't do.

The same is true with Sunday School teaching. Many teachers spend sufficient time studying the Bible. They know what God has said, they understand scriptural principles, and they can explain what God expects us to do. But they dump everything into one big kettle; they present their material in a poorly prepared, disorganized manner. Consequently, no one wants seconds (or firsts, either).

Really good teachers, however, take time to plan the presentation of their lesson. They know that the presentation is crucial, and they work out that element of their lesson carefully. They take great pains to eliminate distractions—such as noise, poor lighting, uncomfortable chairs, and crowded classrooms—that would hinder effective communication.

It also is helpful to recognize another tip. Many teachers find it quite effective to plan their lesson in the *reverse* order of how it will be presented in class. They first plan the ending, then the middle portion, and finally the beginning. Let's look at each of these planning phases.

Phase One: Planning Desired Responses

While it may seem odd to begin at the end, many teachers find this the best way to prepare a Sunday School lesson plan. Of course, having spent adequate time in Bible study, you already know the facts and the principles of the passage you're teaching. But after the basic building blocks of the lesson are determined, they should be arranged and prepared in such a way that you will accomplish the desired outcome. That outcome, naturally, will be the changed behavior of your learners; after all, the purpose of teaching is to help students become what God wants them to be and to do what God wants them to do.

This change in a learner's behavior, then, should be the stated aim or objective of your teaching. It is important to recognize that good aims relate to affecting your learners' behavior, not only their knowledge. There is nothing wrong with wanting learners to *know* something, but teaching should achieve more than knowledge divorced from action.

Consider the following aims. A "knowledge aim" from the lesson about Jericho might be to share what God told the Israelites to do at Jericho. That certainly would be a valid aim, but it is limited to the facts of the biblical account. It is an exposition of ancient history. A better aim is to address the importance of obedience and how God blesses those who follow Him. This is a much stronger aim, because it stresses principles which are valid for today.

But the best type of aim addresses the behavior of the learners. A "behavorial aim" would emphasize the fact that learners should obey God in the same way that the Israelites obeyed Him at the city of Jericho. This approach covers the Bible facts, but also includes an explanation of what learners should do to apply Bible principles to life. This aim could be made even stronger by suggesting specific ways that learners could practice obedience ("Obey your parents this week by hanging up your clothes each day"). This "behavior aim" could be coupled with a "knowledge aim" such as "We must obey our parents, even as the Israelites obeyed God at Jericho."

A teacher is well along the way to having a good lesson plan when he has stated clear, concise, and appropriate aims. Good aims describe both what your learners should *know* and what they should *do*. I've found that a good approach is to have *two* aims for each lesson. One of these could emphasize the principles which learners should know when the class session is over. The second should indicate the type of the behavior their newfound knowledge ought to produce.

At this point, you're probably wondering how to determine what aims you should emphasize. One way is to select aims that can be evaluated or measured. That way, you can determine whether your students' behavior actually is changing. In the example above, your students could report back at the beginning of the next lesson to tell you how many times they hung up their clothes. A learner who did it once has made progress. If he did it twice in the following week, he has done twice as well. Both parents and children could measure achievement and progress. And that's what Sunday School teaching is all about—helping learners progress from where they are, to where God wants them to be.

Phase Two: Planning Discovery Methods

We now move backward from the desired learner response to the body of the lesson. In the lesson itself, a teacher must use effective methods to help students discover both the facts and the principles of the Word. As we noted before, almost any Bible portion contains far more facts and princples than you could cover in a given class session. But unless you have determined your aims, you will have a problem knowing which aspects of the passage to emphasize.

However, once you *do* know what facts and principles you will emphasize, choosing good methods is greatly simplified. For guidelines in selecting methods, refer to chapters 5 and 6 of this book. Just remember that the best methodology is the one which gets learners involved in the teaching/learning process. Methodology should stimulate active, not passive involvement.

Phase Three: Planning to Make Contact

Now we have moved all the way back to the beginning of the lesson. Since you have determined aims that relate to knowing biblical principles and changing behavior (phase one), you've been able to select the appropriate methods to help learners discover these facts and principles (phase two). Now you are ready to determine how you should focus your students' attention. Remember that they come from widely diverse backgrounds and experiences. You need to plan a point of contact to bring them to the place where they will want to discover what God has to say about their behavior.

The point of contact can be chosen from a wide variety of activities. If your previous class session included specific "action aims," you might want to begin there. Allowing learners to share what God has done in their lives can be a very stimulating experience. Or, if they're having problems applying what they've been studying, encourage them to voice their feelings. It is important, however, that you guide this discussion time so that it relates to the lesson you plan to cover presently.

Also, don't ever assume that you have a class full of highly motivated learners. They may or may not be. You should begin, though, by assuming that what you do at the *opening* of the class session will determine whether you're able to establish contact with your learners. When you begin to teach a new class, you may be confronted with a group of unenthusiastic learners. But this can change. If you've followed this book's suggestions, they will recognize that you have studied the Bible diligently and are well prepared to teach. When you have chosen aims that relate to what they need, and when they become excited about discovering biblical truths, they will become more highly motivated.

When students expect something meaningful to happen in class, they will come prepared to learn. Then you will know the excitement of being used of God to help learners grow and mature as He desires. It will be a thoroughly invigorating experience. You may never be the same again!

Application Activities

(1) How many times do you think you could read through a typical lesson's Scripture passage? If you were to spread your reading over five or six days in the week, how many times could you read it each day?

_____

_____

_____

(2) Why are so many teachers willing to settle for "knowlege

aims" in their instruction rather than "life response aims"?

_____

_____

_____

(3) Examine a Sunday School teacher's manual (either your own, or borrow one from another teacher). In your opinion, does it stress biblical principles, or does it simply focus on facts?

_____

_____

_____

(4) Why is it a good idea to plan your lesson by starting at the end of your presentation, considering the outcomes you expect?

_____

_____

_____

_____

_____

CHAPTER ELEVEN
TEACHING WITH SKILL

Don't ever teach if you can find a legitimate reason not to. Perhaps that's a strange way to end a book on teaching, but I mean it. Don't ever think that you *must* become a Sunday School teacher. God does not expect all of us to teach. As Paul observes:

> For just as we have many members in one body and all the members do not have the same function, so we, who are many, are one body in Christ, and individually members one of another. And since we have gifts that differ according to the grace given to us, let each exercise them accordingly (Rom. 12:4-6).

A great misunderstanding seems to be prevalent in many churches. Some people espouse the idea that all Christians should have the same spiritual gifts. But I am convinced that God has blessed each of us with specific gifts to be used to carry out whatever responsibility He has given us. Therefore, it would be far better for a person not to teach at all, than to serve without feeling that he or she has a gift for it.

It also is important to note that those of us who teach are accountable to God for our actions. For this reason James warned that we should not covet a teaching position:

> Let not many of you become teachers, my brethren, knowing that we shall incur a stricter judgment (James 3:1).

God apparently has expectations for teachers that exceed His demands for others. This is logical, for a teacher not only is responsible for his own behavior, but in some degree, for that of his students. In the very next verse, James indicates that all of us are prone to stumble, and that one of our sensitive areas is our everyday speech (3:2). Because of the volume of verbal communication involved in teaching, teachers are particularly vulnerable in this area.

But because of the importance of teaching, we should seek to discover if God has given us a gift for it. The best way to discover if we possess that gift may be to *try* teaching. In my opinion, many more Christians have the gift of teaching than think they do. Over the years I have encountered many, many Christians who never knew that God had given them teaching gifts. But when they ventured out, with very little instruction, it immediately became obvious that in God's eyes, they had been teachers all along!

I remember a dear Christian lady in a church where I was serving as Minister of Education. Charlotte had been an excellent musician—a vocal soloist. But as she grew older, she found that her voice became less dependable. So she began to look for other ways to serve the Lord.

After I announced that I was going to hold a training class for prospective Sunday School teachers, Charlotte met me in the hall. She recounted her commitment to the Lord and explained that she had served through the years by singing to His glory. Since she felt that her vocal abilities had diminished, she thought perhaps she should look into teaching. I explained that taking this training class was not an agreement to teach, but merely an opportunity to investigate the possibility. Nonetheless, she attended all the sessions faithfully.

After the final training class we talked together. Charlotte agreed that she would like to try the next step—working with another teacher as an assistant. She started the following week and did marvelously.

Finally, the week that she had been waiting for arrived. Charlotte taught the class she had been assisting. After Sunday School on that momentous day, we again met in the hallway. This time she came running up to me; I wasn't quite sure if she was going to hug me or tackle me!

"I did it!" she blurted out. When I inquired as to what it was she had done, Charlotte replied, "I taught this morning! It was wonderful! When can I have a class of my own?" You can imagine my delight. Needless to say we were able to find a class that she could teach regularly.

Throughout her years of walking with the Lord, I suspect that Charlotte *always* had possessed the gift of teaching—or at least the potential for it. But she had never ventured out. She had not tried teaching. But as soon as she did, it was obvious to her, to me, and to her students, that she had a special gift in this area.

Very few people know what their spiritual gifts are until they try various options. While Christians who do not have the gift of teaching should not teach, those who have been gifted by God *must* teach. The body of Christ needs our ministry, and we need to exercise our gifts to God's glory and to our own fulfillment.

Having stated this, let's now summarize the major themes of this book.

Biblical Teachers

We have considered what the Bible says and demonstrates about teaching. It is a vital function in the New Testament church. As we look in the Old Testament, we see that teaching also played a key role in guiding those who would love and serve God. The quality of Israel's spiritual life related directly to the quality of the teaching the Israelites received. When God's Word was taught, the nation was strong. When it was neglected, the nation fell into sin.

So it is in the church today. When the Bible is taught in a way that allows learners to understand and apply godly principles, a church will be strong and vibrant. But when the teaching of the Word is neglected, Christianity becomes a series of forms and rituals with little or no meaning. Few churches are able to minister effectively to their own members and reach out to the unsaved without effective Sunday School teaching.

And, as we have seen in the early chapters of this book, teaching should bring about changes in the lives of the students. Unapplied teaching—instruction that fails to produce change—is not teaching at all. It may be a lecture, it may be a story-telling session, it may even be an action-packed get-together. But until someone has learned, we have not taught.

Finally, as teachers, who and what we are influences our students as much as what we say to them. We are to guide our learners into discovering truth. But even more than that, we are to show them God's truth by our lives. A teacher is an example. We who are teachers should recognize that our spiritual maturity is the goal toward which our students will strive. And it is the Holy Spirit, working through our lives and ministry, who will bring our students to that level.

Motivated Students

In order to learn and grow, students must be motivated. Motivation comes from within and is a function of the learner. But teachers can play a strategic role in triggering that motivation. Our student/teacher relationships and class activities will influence the learners' levels of motivation. Interaction with students outside of class also will reinforce and enhance classtime activities.

Occasionally, we may encounter learners who are highly motivated. They come to us thirsty, and we need only direct them to water. Such students are a delight to a teacher's heart. But this type of individual doesn't come along very often, and we should not count on his or her presence in our class. Rather, we should plan class sessions that will trigger the internal motivation that drives students to seek answers to their deepest questions.

Effective Methods

Effective class sessions are those that get students involved in the teaching/learning process; the more active the involvement, the bettter. Passive students are bored students. And when students are bored, it is unlikely that they will learn very much. Indeed they may come to hate formal learning experiences. Rather than relying on words alone—even interesting ones—we need to look for other channels of communication. We need to involve as many of our students' senses as possible. The more personally involved learners are, the more effective our instruction will be.

In addition to teaching with effective words and multisensory forms of communication, we must strive for dynamic interaction in our teaching. Students who are participating with each other, as well as with the teacher, will profit greatly. Group discussion, question/answer sessions, brainstorming, and other interactive techniques will compound the effectiveness of our teaching. And remember: the more effective our teaching becomes, the greater the spiritual growth we can expect from our students.

Planning Effective Teaching

The effectiveness of what goes on in a classroom usually is determined by what transpires in our preparation and study time. When we are better prepared, our teaching will be better too. The results of our study will produce spiritual fruit as we understand how to communicate in the classroom.

One simple approach to teaching is the three-step sequence presented earlier. The first step, making contact with our students, will focus students' attention on the lesson. We all come to a Sunday School class with a variety of concerns clamoring for our attention. The purpose of a lesson's introduction is to draw each person away from those conflicting demands and to direct each one toward the subject at hand. The focus time is crucial to a good class. It involves making contact with students and setting the direction for the class session.

The second step is to discover what God has said in His Word about the topic to be studied. This means going to the Bible to discover both the facts and the principles of the Word. When we have studied and prepared effectively, we will know the facts of the lesson and then find principles in it that can be applied to life. It is our task, as teachers, to guide learners into discovering those, and other, truths. There is no substitute for guided discovery learning. Because it is interesting and effective, it can be life-transforming.

The third step in effective teaching is to help students apply the principles they've discovered. This means planning class activities to give students an opportunity to begin applying God's Word. But application must reach beyond the class session. It must extend out into life. Then we will see the body of Christ growing and maturing.

As a result, we are no longer to be children, tossed here and there by waves, and carried about by every wind of doctrine, by the trickery of men, by craftiness in deceitful scheming;

but speaking the truth in love, we are to grow up in all aspects into Him, who is the head, even Christ, from whom the whole body, being fitted and held together by that which every joint supplies, according to the proper working of each individual part, causes the growth of the body for the building up of itself in love (Eph. 4:14-16).

I recently was worshiping on a Sunday morning with my family. Kevin (age 13) and Nathan (age 11) were sitting on either side of me. Our pastor was preaching from Matthew 6. He was sharing Christ's admonition not to lay up treasures for ourselves on earth, but to seek treasures in heaven.

As the pastor spoke, I felt a tap on my arm and leaned over to hear Nathan whisper, "But he hasn't told us how to do it yet!"

You can imagine my excitement. Not only was my son paying attention, but he was asking a key question: "I've heard what God has said. Now how do I put that message into action?" Our pastor, being a well prepared and effective communicator, went on to suggest how we should lay up treasures in heaven. Later that afternoon, at the dinner table, our entire family discussed specific ways we could set our minds on heavenly things. We even discussed strategies to accomplish this goal.

May all of our teaching be so relevant. May we cultivate a whole generation of learners who are not satisfied with a passive acceptance of instruction. We need students who actively study and learn the Word, and who then go out and live its truths.

As we teach in this way, we also will be answering the question that Nathan asked me on that Sunday morning. How can we establish treasures for ourselves in heaven? We can do so by building up the lives of our students, by helping them to grow and to mature—to become more like Christ.

What is Sunday School all about? Keeping students quiet?

Hardly! Baby-sitting until the adults are finished? Never! Killing time for parents until the children are ready to be picked up? Don't you believe it! A teacher is one who cooperates with the Spirit of God to accomplish His will in the world. Don't ever settle for anything less. Make your teaching count!

CHRISTIAN EDUCATION BOOKS FROM VICTOR

The Art of Recruiting Volunteers *by Mark Senter*
If you've ever had to make dozens of phone calls trying to fill a volunteer position, you'll appreciate this handy, step-by-step guide that can help you avoid recruitment problems tactfully (6-2297).

Building a Caring Church *by Tom and Janie Lovorn*
Does your church have a heart? Has your desire to meet people's needs in Jesus' name moved from theory to consistent practice? Tom and Janie Lovorn offer creative, pretested ideas you can use to help make your church a caring church (6-2150).

The Church Education Handbook *by Kenneth O. Gangel*
This book offers a broad view of 48 aspects of church education, including such topics as solving the absentee problem, operating a C.E. Board, delegating effectively, and much, much more (6-2602).

Evaluate and Grow *by Harold J. Westing*
Is your Sunday School's rate of growth dwindling? These proven measuring sticks will help you evaluate your program and get your Sunday School growing again (6-2624).

The Holy Spirit in Your Teaching *by Roy B. Zuck*
If you'd like to experience less of the frustration of teaching and more of the joy, read what Dr. Zuck has to say about spiritual dynamics in Bible instruction (6-2622).

24 Ways to Improve Your Teaching by Kenneth O. Gangel
Each class differs in interests, attention span, and mental ability. In this book, you'll learn 24 unique teaching techniques—everything from buzz groups to role playing. Dr. Gangel's insights will add variety to your teaching (6-2235).